RON ARMSTRONG

D1572379

More TO THIS LIFE

LIVING the LIFE YOU WERE CREATED FOR

REDEMPTION PRESS

Published by Redemption Press, PO Box 427, Enumclaw, WA 98022.

Toll-Free (844) 2REDEEM (273-3336)

Redemption Press is honored to present this title in partnership with the author. The views expressed or implied in this work are those of the author. Redemption Press provides our imprint seal representing design excellence, creative content, and high-quality production.

Scripture quotations marked NIV are taken from the Holy Bible, New International Version®, NIV® Copyright ©1973, 1978, 1984, 2011 by Biblica, Inc.® Used by permission. All rights reserved worldwide.

Names used with permission.

ISBN: 978-1-64645-113-5 (Paperback)
978-1-64645-114-2 (ePub)
978-1-64645-115-9 (Mobi)

Library of Congress Catalog Card Number: 2020910929

Contents

Acknowledgments

Many people have contributed to my life and this book in one way or another throughout the years.

First and foremost, I would like to thank my wife Teresa and our children Ryan and Breanna for supporting me and allowing me to lead our family in the direction God has called us through the years. There were many exciting as well as challenging seasons in our family life, and you were great troopers through it all.

I grew up in the Valley Assembly of God Church in Spokane Valley, Washington, where I attended for thirty years. It was during my teenage years that Pastor Everett Olp was pastoring along with his two sons, Tim and Tom. I greatly appreciate the roles that each one of them played during that season in my life. I owe them a debt of gratitude for their investment in me.

I would like to thank Pastor Al Hulten for providing me the season of preparation for ministry and his mentorship while I was at Valley Assembly of God and Pastor Fred Pace for being a mentor and friend to me in my early years of ministry at Suncrest Family Worship Center. I would also like to thank my board members at MeadowWood Christian Center and Suncrest Family Worship Center for believing in me, challenging me, and supporting me.

If it wasn't for my mother's example of what a relationship with Jesus looks like and her prayers for me, I wouldn't be the person I am today. I also greatly appreciate my dad showing and teaching me a hard work ethic.

Every one of these people, and more, have all contributed to me personally and to my life's calling and work.

Lastly and most importantly, I would like to thank the Lord for his faithfulness to me and my family through every season of our lives. He has always provided for us and taken care of us through these adventurous years of following Him, and that adventure is far from over.

Thank you Lord, for all you have taught me through the years in and out of ministry and inspiring me to write this book so that others might be blessed and challenged to live the life you created them for.

Introduction

*"I have come that they may have life,
and have it to the full." (Jesus)*
John 10:10

People are always searching for more. No matter what our position or status in life, there is still something inside of us that yearns for more. More love in our relationships, more peace in our heart and home, more joy in our life, more money in our bank account or retirement fund, more intimacy in our marriage, more of God's grace and favor in our life, more time off, more time spent doing the things we love to do, more of the things that add to our life—whatever that represents for you. There is a danger, however, in not finding contentment with what we have or where we are in life. We *think* some pursuits in life will bring us greater fulfillment or happiness, but in reality, they leave us empty inside.

There is more to this life than your economic status, climbing the corporate ladder or your physical appearance. There is still "more" that God has for each of us that we have yet to experience in this life. What that more consists of can be similar as well as vastly different from person to person. We could all use more intimacy with Jesus, for example, but what God is calling me to will be different than his call on your life.

When I look at the lives of the Israelites and the land God had promised his people, I see God had so much more for them than what they were living. They went from living in a land of bondage to wandering in the desert, but God had a place of abundance for them that they had yet to experience represented in a "land flowing with milk and honey." In the same way, Jesus has so much more for us that we have yet to experience. After all, Jesus came to give us an abundant and full life (Jn. 10:10).

I learned firsthand many years ago that God's plan for my life was greater than the plans I had for my own life. He has so much more for me than I ever imagined for myself, and he does for you as well.

God has a plan for your life. His plan involves much more than what you now experience. He wants you to have the full and abundant life found in Jesus Christ. Jesus is the Giver of life. Life without him is empty, void, and meaningless. Life without him is no life at all. Only he can bring you true and lasting fulfillment. Only he can give you life—abundant and eternal.

One day after reading the words "'For I know the plans I have for you,' declares the Lord," found in Jeremiah 29:11, I was feeling frustrated because I thought I knew the plans God had for me. After complaining to the Lord that those plans were not working out, he spoke very clearly to me saying, "I know the plans I have for you. You don't!" Looking back now, I can see that I didn't even have a clue what God had planned for my life.

You can experience more in life by taking hold of all God's plans for you, just as the Israelites experienced more when they took possession of the promised land. From God's promise to Abraham to its fulfillment through Joshua, God's people took hold of the land through their relationship with him. Each of the principles we'll discuss here apply to the individual Christian as well as the church. Through these principles, God will bring you to the very place he has destined for you.

God's plan consists of his calling on your life. He wants to use you to fulfill his kingdom plans, so he has given you a specific place in Christ. As God led the Israelites on their journey to their promised land, he leads you on a journey to your personal promises through a relationship with him.

This journey is not just about getting somewhere or taking hold of something. It's also about a journey with someone—Jesus himself. It's about Jesus fulfilling his plans for you, in you, and through you. So I challenge and encourage you to take that journey to experience the more you were created for.

Chapter One

Living God's Divine Perspective

*When the angel of the Lord appeared to Gideon, he said,
"The Lord is with you, mighty warrior."*
Judges 6:12

JUDGES 6–7

Some people may feel like their life doesn't amount to much. They may think they are insignificant. They may feel like their life consists only of existing day to day. They feel helpless when it comes to their struggles in life. They feel hopeless, wondering if their life will ever change.

No matter who you are, where you've been, or what you've done, God has a purpose for you. Just because you may not be popular, have a certain grade point average, athletic ability, or education doesn't mean God can't use you or doesn't have a purpose for your life. On the contrary, he has instilled in you specific gifts to fulfill his purpose in your life.

Many years ago, while I was studying for the ministry, I had in mind what I wanted that ministry to look like. I had my position picked out, and I had a vision for my life. When I got the opportunity to step into that position, I knew it was for me. But it didn't take the Lord long to show me this was not his plan.

My disappointment ran deep. I'd been sure this was God's will. It was the desire of my heart. It made perfect sense. I was already doing volunteer ministry at Valley Assembly of God in Spokane, Washington, where I had attended most of my life. Now they offered me a full-time position as children's pastor.

I had longed for the day when the Lord would open a door for me to enter full-time ministry. In my mind, this was it. But my wife, Teresa, didn't feel right about it. Believe me, I pleaded my case with her, but she stood her ground. I knew I couldn't move forward if she didn't believe this was God's will.

As I sat in my truck before work one day, expressing my disappointment to God, he spoke clearly to me. "If I were to tell you the plans I have for you, you wouldn't believe it."

So I broke the news to my pastor, Al Hulten, who then told me about another church, Suncrest Family Worship Center, that was looking for a children's pastor and thought I should consider it.

I met with the pastor of Suncrest Family Worship Center in Nine Mile Falls, Washington, (a community outside of Spokane) and knew that this was where God was leading us. God used my wife and Pastor Al Hulten to show my family and me that this is where he would have us go. I knew at that time that his plans for my life were much greater than I had planned for myself, but I still didn't know what they were. I was excited to see what God had in store for me.

Living through God's divine perspective on your life through a relationship with Jesus Christ will bring you fulfillment. The things of this world will never fulfill you like a personal relationship with Jesus.

In Judges chapter 6, the Midianites had overtaken and oppressed God's people, the Israelites. At this time in Israel's history, they possessed the land God had promised them. But they didn't live in true possession of the land because they weren't living for God, and this led to their oppression. This enemy nation had impoverished the Israelites, so they cried out to the Lord for help. God answered their cry by raising up Gideon to save them from the hands of the Midianites.

God Longs to Be in Your Life

> When the angel of the Lord appeared to Gideon, he said, "The Lord is with you, mighty warrior."
>
> "But sir," Gideon replied, "if the Lord is with us, why has all this happened to us? Where are all his wonders that our fathers told us about when they said, 'Did not the Lord bring us up out of Egypt?' But now the Lord has abandoned us and put us into the hand of Midian."
>
> The Lord turned to him and said, "Go in the strength you have and save Israel out of Midian's hand. Am I not sending you?"
>
> "But Lord," Gideon asked, "how can I save Israel? My clan is the weakest in Manasseh, and I am the least in my family." (Judg. 6:12–15)

The first thing the angel of the Lord says to Gideon is, "The Lord is with you (v. 12). Gideon then responds, "If the Lord is with us, then why has all of this happened to us?" (v. 13). Maybe you have asked yourself a similar question: "If God is with me, if

God loves me, if there is a God, why has he allowed bad things to happen to me?"

I remember a season when everything went from bad to worse with my job. One day, I came home distraught, beside myself. I couldn't go on another day. I was working as a bus driver for over three years at this point, and after a series of events and frustrations, a fender bender that day was the breaking point for me.

That evening, I received another job offer.

It was the greatest relief I'd felt in a long time. The Lord used all the horrible aspects of my job to move me into a new career. If I'd been satisfied with my job, I probably wouldn't have considered the new position. My present job paid well and had great benefits. It would have made perfect sense to stay where I was, even though I didn't like the position. But God had other plans and used those circumstances to lead me to something better. God will use your difficulties, pain, and suffering for his greater purposes for your life. The positive side of that position was that the Lord used it to lead me into a ministry to underprivileged people that I am still involved in to this day.

God has seen everything that has happened to you, good and bad, whether you brought them on yourself or not. He knows all the wrong choices you've made, and he still loves you. He has been by your side. He has seen your tears. He has felt your pain. Nothing has been hidden from his sight. He has been there, even though you haven't seen him or felt his presence. If you are a Christian, God works in your life even if you don't see or feel him working. If you are not in a right relationship with God, he's been trying to get your attention. But you keep him out by going your own way.

The Lord has always been aware of every aspect of your life, yet he longs to be in it. When you invite Jesus Christ to be your Lord and Savior, you open your life to him, allowing him to work. He wants to forgive your sins. He wants to heal your hurt. He wants to comfort you in your pain. He even works through your difficult circumstances to draw you to him.

Even if you are not a Christian, God is aware of everything that has taken place in your life. He longs for you to repent of your sins and turn to him. He wants to work in your life.

Jesus loves you so much, and he wants to have a personal relationship with you. He died on the cross to make that relationship possible. The Bible says, "For God so loved the world that he gave his one and only Son, that whoever believes in him shall not perish, but have eternal life" (Jn. 3:16). His death on the cross was a demonstration of his love for you. "But God demonstrates his own love for us in this: While we were still sinners, Christ died for us" (Rom. 5:8). The Bible says we have all sinned, and that sin has separated us from God. "For all have sinned and fall short of the glory of God" (Rom. 3:23). "The wages of sin is death, but the gift of God is eternal life through Jesus Christ our Lord" (Rom. 6:23). That death is not just a physical death, but a spiritual one. Sin brought death, and death results in separation.

If you've ever been to an open-casket funeral, you have seen the body of the deceased person. Their body is there, but you can no longer have a relationship with that person. You can't have a conversation with them. Why? Because their death resulted in separation from you. That's what happened because of our sin. We died spiritually, which resulted in our separation from God.

The good news is that Jesus died on the cross for your sins and rose again to bring you back into a right relationship with him. Our sin had to be paid for, but we couldn't pay it ourselves. So Jesus paid it for us, through his death on the cross.

But Jesus's death on the cross doesn't automatically save us. He provided for the forgiveness of our sins. He provided for our salvation. It's up to us to turn to him in faith. John 1:12 says, "Yet to all who received him, to those who believed in his name, he gave the right to become children of God." The way we receive him is by personal invitation. "For everyone who calls on the name of the Lord will be saved" (Rom. 10:13). At that point, you become what the Bible calls "born again" (Jn. 3:3). This means your spirit, dead because of sin, is made alive again by the Holy Spirit (Titus 3:5).

Jesus died on the cross to make it possible for you to have a relationship with him. If you open your life to him by confessing that you are a sinner and want him to be your Lord and Savior, he will forgive all your sins and give you a brand-new start in life. When we make Jesus our Lord, we commit to living for him rather than our own sinful, selfish desires. It's not a matter of working for your salvation but walking out your salvation. You are saved from your sins when you turn to faith in Jesus. You walk out that salvation by living in obedience to his Word and his will for your life. Some people just want Jesus to be their Savior, but not their Lord. They want the forgiveness of their sins and to be assured of heaven, but they continue to live a life of sin. Jesus needs to be your Lord and Savior. It's a package deal. Eternal life is a gift of God, but it's through Jesus Christ our LORD (Rom. 6:23).

If you want to make Jesus the Lord and Savior of your life, then commit your life to him by praying this prayer to him. "Jesus, I am a sinner in need of your forgiveness. I believe you died on the cross for my sins and you rose again and are alive today. Come into my life. Be my Lord and Savior. I dedicate my life to following you by living according to your Word and your will for my life. Thank you for dying for me, for forgiving me, and for saving me. Amen."

If you just prayed that prayer, you have become a child of God and have a new life. One way God speaks to us is through his Word, the Bible. Begin reading the Bible every day. The book of John is a good place to start. Choose a translation you can understand.

Begin talking to God on a regular basis. Talk to him as you would talk to a friend. Ask him for his help in the big and small things in your life, in the challenges you face. Find a good church that teaches the Bible. There you can make Christian friends and grow in your walk with the Lord. And tell someone about your decision for Jesus. Perhaps a Christian you know has been praying for you. If so, let them know what you've done. They can help you get started in your new relationship with Jesus.

Whether you have been a Christian for many years or just now committed your life to Christ, begin living through God's divine perspective on your life.

God Has a Greater Call on Your Life

The second thing the angel of the Lord said to Gideon was that he was a "mighty warrior" (Judg. 6:12). Gideon probably looked around to make sure the angel wasn't talking to someone else and said, "You've got to be kidding? Me? I'm just a local boy working on the family farm, threshing wheat. Mighty warrior? You have the wrong person."

God saw Gideon in light of who he was to become, in light of God's plans for his life. God saw Gideon as a mighty warrior because that is what God had planned for his life, to be a mighty warrior and save Israel out of the Midianites' hands. Gideon underestimated God's purpose for his life. He did not see himself as God saw him.

I'm sure King David never imagined himself as someday becoming the king of all Israel. As a shepherd boy, he'd learned to fight off lions and bears, which prepared him to take down Goliath. Then, in time, God moved him into the kingship. Joseph also went through some long and difficult years as God prepared him to become governor of Egypt.

You may think you're a nobody and your life amounts to nothing. But God has a plan and purpose for you. He sees who he wants you to become and what he has planned for your life. Don't underestimate his purposes. Whatever you have planned for your life, God's plans are even better.

The Lord may call you to a position in the secular world, or he may call you to the ministry as a vocation. If you're not sure of your calling, ask God to begin stirring your heart in the direction he wants you to move. He will give you desires that fall in line with his plans for you. Having a desire to do something doesn't always mean God is calling you to that place or position. Test the desire by giving it to God and asking him either to take away the desire or make it grow. As with Gideon, your weakness or insecurity might be where God is calling you. It was for me.

When I was a teenager, I never thought I would someday be a pastor or evangelist, preaching his Word. I kept to myself. I never went out for sports after the seventh grade. I worked in my dad's business. I hated speaking in a group setting. I never dreamed of the things God had planned for my life. The Lord made my purpose evident to me years ago: to revitalize the church and evangelize the lost by preaching God's Word and through the power of the Holy Spirit. You can become anything God has planned for you. You were born for a purpose, and he will fulfill that purpose as you walk in obedience and relationship with him.

Take Steps of Faith

In verse 15 Gideon asks, "But Lord, how can I save Israel? My clan is the weakest in Manasseh and I am the least in my family." In other words, Gideon says, "I have no credentials. I have no degree. I come from a family of nobodies, and I am the biggest nobody of them all. How can I save Israel?" The Lord says, "Go in the strength you have. I will be with you." Gideon was to go in faith that the Lord would enable him to do what he called him to do.

God has given you a call and commission beyond your capabilities. You need his grace, wisdom, power, and presence to live out his purpose. Without him, you cannot become who he wants you to be.

Begin by taking steps of faith. If you do not have Jesus Christ in your life, the first step of faith is offering your life totally and completely to him and inviting him to be your Lord and Savior. Then whatever God calls you to do, take steps of faith toward that call. By the stirring in your heart and the confirmation of his Word, you'll know what God is calling you to do. If you feel God may be calling to do something, ask him to confirm it to you. When you know he is leading you to do something specific, to take that step of faith, go in the strength you have. He will be with you. He will empower you and give you the ability to do whatever he calls you to do.

Whatever God calls you to do will be a step of faith because you don't know the outcome. Some steps of faith are greater than others, depending on the consequences. Leaving a job, for example, would have greater consequences than talking to someone about Jesus. The one could leave you unemployed, the other one less friend. But if God is in it, the outcome will be what he wants it to be. Leave the results to him. He will honor your step of faith.

Reach Others Who Need Jesus

God called Gideon to save Israel out of the enemy's hand. When you come to faith in Christ, the Lord saves you out of the grasp of Satan, who has been holding you captive to do his will (2 Tim. 2:26). When Jesus saves you, it isn't just so you can live a better life. Jesus saves us to live in relationship with him and to reach others who need him.

I've heard people say that God has not called us to save people, just to love them. Yes, loving them is central to reaching them, but love alone will not save them if that love doesn't point them to Jesus. Ultimately, we can't save anyone. Only God can. But we sometimes use that mindset to release ourselves from our responsibility to reach the lost, which God has called us to do. Jesus said, "I have come to seek and save the lost" (Jn. 4:10). Jesus also told his disciples, "As the Father has sent me, I am sending you" (Jn. 20:21).

The Lord told the apostle Paul, "I am sending you to open their eyes and turn them from darkness to light and from the power of Satan to God" (Acts 26:18). It's also what he told Gideon: "Am I not sending you?" And Jesus commissioned us all to "go and make disciples of all nations" (Matt. 28:19–20).

When we come to faith in Christ, he commissions and sends us to reach others who are lost and held captive by the devil. God's call to you is to come and follow him as your Lord and Savior. God's commission to you is to reach others who need Jesus in their life. Yes, that requires loving them, but loving them is only one element to saving and discipling them.

Evangelism is necessary if we are to reach people for Christ. Discipleship is necessary to grow people in Christ. As disciples ourselves, we need to grow in our relationship with Christ as well as evangelize the lost and help them grow in their relationship with Christ. Evangelism and discipleship go hand in hand. As followers of Christ, we evangelize and disciple others. That's the Great Commission.

Who in your sphere of influence needs Jesus? What can you do to influence them for Christ? Those are the people God has placed in your life so you could reach them for him. Build a bridge of relationship with them and prayerfully consider ways to show and share Christ with them.

Expect God to Empower You

> Then the Spirit of the Lord came upon Gideon, and he blew a trumpet, summoning the Abiezrites to follow him. He sent messengers throughout Manasseh, calling them to arms, and also into Asher, Zebulun and Naphtali, so that they too went up to meet them. (Judg. 6:34–36)

When Gideon went in the strength he had, "the Spirit of the Lord came upon Gideon" (6:34). It was after he took a step of faith, God empowered him to do what he'd called and commissioned him to do. That was one confirmation to Gideon that God was with him and would see him through.

When you take a step of faith by turning your life over to Jesus, by his Spirit, God will enable you to live for him and carry out his call and commission. Turning your life over to Jesus is only the first of many steps of faith you will take in your Christian walk. If you think the Christian life is boring, it's because you haven't taken steps of faith. On the contrary, the Christian life is the most exciting and exhilarating life. You'll discover this truth when you begin taking steps of faith that require risk.

Satan is going to do everything in his power to keep you from turning to faith in Christ and from taking steps of faith. He doesn't want you to experience all that God has planned for you, so he'll use doubt, fear, unbelief, temptation, and distractions to try to stop you. If you haven't made Jesus your Lord and Savior, Satan will use all those and more to keep you from making that decision. If you are a Christian, he will use all those things and more to keep you from experiencing all God has for you.

Without Jesus, you live under the control of the devil. But it doesn't have to be that way. God has the power to break the devil's hold on you. Jesus came to set the captive free (Lk. 4:18). Your freedom is found in Jesus Christ. When you invite Jesus into your life, he sets you free from the devil's hold on your life. If you have not surrendered your life to Jesus Christ, the devil has been holding you captive to do his will, whether you realize it or not. But Jesus wants to set you free.

Expect God to Use You

Gideon started out with 32,000 men in his army to fight the Midianites (7:3). God told him he had too many. After sifting through the troops, Gideon ended up with only 300 men (7:7). And with those 300 men, Gideon defeated the Midianites with God's help.

When God empowers you to do what he calls you to do, you can expect him to use you to do amazing things in and through you. Gideon had minimal resources. He and his small army had trumpets, jars, and torches. They didn't have anything you would expect an army to have, like spears and shields. And yet, that's all God needed.

No matter how limited your resources are or how ill equipped you feel, God will use what you have to do amazing things in and through your life. Expect great things from God. He will do amazing things in your family, your friends, your school or workplace, and your community through your influence. Our God is an amazing God. Everything he does is amazing. He will amaze you by the work he will do. He is calling you to live out his divine perspective on your life. Gideon did and so can you.

Reflection

1. Have you been born again, inviting Jesus into your life to be your Lord and Savior? If so, tell someone what led you to open your life to Christ.
2. Is God calling you to do something you've had on your heart to accomplish for him?
3. What do you think could be the "greater call" God has placed on your life?
4. What next step of faith can you take toward experiencing "more?"
5. Identify one person in your life who needs Jesus. What can you do to influence them for him?
6. What "little" do you have that God could use (gifts, talents, money, etc.)?

Encouragement: If you have decided to follow Jesus and make him your Lord and Savior, you are now a child of God. If you've decided to take evangelism and discipleship to the next level, he will be with you and help you. He is your strength.

Challenge: The next time you feel discouraged, disheartened, or defeated, give those negative feelings to Jesus and keep moving forward. God created you for a purpose, and like Gideon, you can live out God's divine perspective on your life as you continue to walk with Him.

Prayer: *Lord Jesus,* thank you for your love for me and the life you have given me. Help me to have your perspective on my life and to live my life through your eyes. I believe your plans for me are much greater than my own. Please stir my heart with your plans for me. Show me the steps of faith you're calling me to take. Place on my heart that one person I can begin to reach for you. Help me to love them and ultimately lead them to you. Use my "little" to accomplish a lot for your glory. Amen.

Chapter Two

Possessing God's Unfailing Promise

Then Caleb silenced the people before Moses and said,
"We should go up and take possession of the land,
for we can certainly do it."
Numbers 13:30

NUMBERS 13–14

God has given you a promise for your life so you can possess it. It's not a promise that you hope will someday come true in your life. It's a guarantee if you meet the conditions to obtain it.

Every time my wife and I hear someone on TV say, "I promise you," when their promise is completely out of their control, we jokingly say, "There they go again, making a promise they can't keep."

We all try our best to keep our promises, or at least we should. But sometimes we fail to do so.

Only one person always keeps his promises: God himself. God promised to lead the Israelites into a good and spacious land, but because of their unbelief and disobedience, an entire generation did not see that promise fulfilled. It's not because God didn't keep his promise. It's because Israel didn't meet the conditions to see its fulfillment. God did fulfill his promise, however, to the next generation.

Believe God's Promise to You by Trusting His Leading

> The Lord said to Moses, "Send some men to explore the land of Canaan, which I am giving to the Israelites. From each ancestral tribe send one of its leaders." (Num. 13:1–2)

> So they went up and explored the land from the Desert of Zin as far as Rehob, toward Lebo Hamath. (Num. 13:21)

When God promised to give the land of Canaan to the Israelites, the whole nation trusted his leading. This was an encouraging promise that God gave to Israel. I'm sure they were excited about it. We all like God's promises. They are good. They give us something to hang onto, and they stir up hope for the future. We get excited about them. We picture what the fulfillment of the promise will look like or how it's going to come about. That's where the Israelites are in this passage. They know Canaan is a land flowing with milk and honey. They know it's a good and spacious place because God already told them so (Ex. 3:8).

After God told me he was calling me to something greater than the first ministry position I was offered, he told me where he wanted me to go and what position I would fill there. I was still working at my fulltime job and volunteering as children's pastor of Suncrest Family Worship Center. One morning, in my devotional time, the Lord made it clear that I would someday be the lead pastor of this church. I was humbled but excited about it. For several years, the Lord gave me opportunities to minister in a realm outside the position I held in that church. This time of growth and on-the-job training prepared me for the position God had promised me.

After much time had passed, a good friend of mine from the church, Bob Hesselgesser, and I went to a men's conference. For some time, I had prayed for God to speak to me there. A significant amount of time had passed since the Lord told me he was calling me to pastor the church I was in, but nothing was happening. So I needed to hear from the Lord. The conference ended and I had no word from the Lord.

On the drive home, Bob said, "I believe God is calling you to pastor our church."

That was the word I needed to hear from God. I went on to explain to Bob that God had placed that very same thing on my heart and that his word was a confirmation to me.

Later, the Lord opened a door for me to become the lead pastor at another church, MeadowWood Christian Center in Liberty Lake, Washington. So I left the church I was in and moved my family. It didn't make sense at the time, but I knew this was God's leading. Several years after that, God led me back to Suncrest Family Worship Center to be the lead pastor there, fulfilling the promise he'd given me many years prior. God gave me a promise, confirmed it through Bob, and fulfilled it years later.

To believe God's promise to you, you must trust his leading. His promise may come to you through his Word, through another person, or in his still, small voice. But however it comes, he will confirm it to you by another means. That is how you test a word from the Lord. If you feel you have received a promise from the Lord, ask him to confirm it. He always does.

You need to decide beforehand that, no matter what God calls you to do, you will do it. No matter what circumstances you face, you will trust him. No matter the cost, you will trust him. No matter how painful it might become, you will trust him. That's what it means to trust God's leading in your life. You follow him, despite your feelings and circumstances. Joseph had a promise from God, but he went through trials, temptations, and even imprisonment. He probably questioned God through some of those difficult times. Yet he remained faithful and ultimately saw God's promise fulfilled.

Move Toward the Calling of God on Your Life, Regardless of Impossibilities

> They came back to Moses and Aaron and the whole Israelite community at Kadesh in the Desert of Paran. There they reported to them and to the whole assembly and showed them the fruit of the land. They gave Moses this account: "We went into the land to which you sent us, and it does flow with milk and honey! Here is its fruit. But the people who live there are powerful, and the cities are fortified and very large. We even saw descendants of Anak there. The Amalekites live in the Negev; the Hittites, Jebusites and Amorites live in the hill country; and the Canaanites live near the sea and along the Jordan." Then Caleb silenced the people before Moses and said, "We should go up and take possession of the land, for we can certainly do it." But the men who had gone up with him said, "We can't attack those people; they are stronger than we are." (Num. 13:26–31)

Why did God want them to explore the land? Why didn't he just send them all over at once to possess it? First, he wanted them to see for themselves that it was a land "flowing with milk and honey," that it was a "good and spacious land." Then he wanted them to see they would have to fight for it. God didn't supernaturally wipe out the inhabitants of the land. Israel had to believe God for it and then go fight for it.

You'll have to fight to possess God's promises too. The enemy isn't going to step aside and surrender. Obtaining God's promise will take backbone and effort as you add fight to your faith.

Ten spies didn't want to fight for God's promise because they thought victory was impossible. They'd heard God's promise to give them the land, but they refused to believe they could conquer the giants.

We'll always be faced with impossibilities—giants that stand between us and God's promise. If we weren't, we wouldn't see our need for God or his help.

When the Lord showed me that he was calling me to be lead pastor of my own church, I had to face and fight the giants of fear and inadequacy. I didn't feel ready to step into that calling. Nevertheless, I moved forward toward that call by continuing my education and doing what God was calling me to do.

God's promise and calling are greater than you. It will look impossible because it is. But his power will enable you to step into his promise, because he will do the work through you. Do not focus on the impossibilities. Focus on God's power and promise.

Move toward the Calling of God, Despite Naysayers

Those ten spies turned the entire community from the promise of God. If the people had listened to Joshua and Caleb instead, the outcome would have been different—only the ten spies would have failed to enter the promised land. The rest of the Israelites would have gone in and possessed the land.

You'll always have naysayers in your life. People will tell you it can't be done, certainly not by you. But those people don't know what God has called you to or promised you. They may have a good reason for doubting. They may even have your best interests at heart. That doesn't mean you shouldn't listen to them or take to heart what they say. Go ahead and hear them out, but disregard whatever does not line up with what God has put in your heart.

When I resigned as lead pastor of MeadowWood Christian Center in Liberty Lake, Washington, back in 2005, some of the leadership and staff tried to talk me out of it. They had a good argument. They didn't want me to leave, and their heart was in the right place. After three and a half years, I had no reason to leave the church and every reason to stay. The Lord had blessed my ministry there. I understood their position, but I also knew what God was leading me to do.

After I left that church, the Lord opened the door for me to return to the church he had promised me I would someday pastor. It was then the Lord fulfilled his promise to me. Even when God calls you to leave something good, you need to follow by obeying his word to you.

Move Forward, Abandoning Fear and Embracing Faith

> That night all the people of the community raised their voices and wept aloud. All the Israelites grumbled against Moses and Aaron, and the whole assembly said to them, "If only we had died in Egypt! Or in this desert! Why is the Lord bringing us to this land only to let us fall by the sword? Our wives and children will be tak-

en as plunder. Wouldn't it be better for us to go back to Egypt?" And they said to each other, "We should choose a leader and go back to Egypt." (Num. 14:1–4)

Ten of the twelve spies gave in to their fears, and Israel followed. They wanted a leader who would take them back to Egypt, to a life of bondage, instead of moving forward into God's promise.

God's promise and calling on your life will scare you to death. It's bigger than you. You can't carry it out in your own strength or ability. The enemy will tempt you to fear your future and turn back or to stay where you are. Don't give in to the fear. Abandon all fear by moving forward in faith. It will take courage, but courage isn't the absence of fear. Courage is moving forward in God's calling in spite of fear.

I learned this lesson on two different occasions when God called me away from fruitful ministries at MeadowWood Christian Center and later Suncrest Family Worship Center, to step into the unknown. It was unknown because I had no idea what would happen next. I had a family to support, and in both cases I didn't know how I was going to do that without having another job lined up. To a certain degree, it was frightening, even though I knew God was in it. But if I wanted to live the life I was created for, I had to abandon my fear and embrace my faith in the Lord, who would be faithful to see me and my family through.

Face the fear, fight the battle, take on the giants, knowing God will go before you and will fight right there alongside you.

The Israelites' unbelief led to disobedience and kept them out of the promised land. Had they embraced faith in the face of fear, that entire generation would have tasted the good and spacious land God had for them.

To embrace faith means to turn your back on your fear and

move forward in what God has called you to do. No matter the obstacle, no matter how insurmountable it may look, no matter how fearful you may feel, embrace faith by taking that next step and believing God.

Reflection

1. What promise do you believe God has given you?
2. In what area in your life do you struggle to trust God completely? Why?
3. What obstacles stand between you and God's promise (for example, doubt, fear, lack of faith, etc.)?
4. Have you listened to a naysayer? How will you move beyond that?
5. Decide now to abandon fear and embrace faith by adding fight to your faith. Begin to pray for God to fulfill his promise to you.

Encouragement: No matter who or what has stood in the way of God's promise to you, and no matter how much time has passed, God is still in the game. He will help you move forward again.

Challenge: Forget the past, forget the regrets, forget the mistakes. Look forward to the future. God doesn't live in your past, and neither should you. He lives in your present and will lead you into your future.

Prayer: *Thank you, Lord,* for your promises. Help me to hear your promise to me, to move forward, regardless of the obstacles before me and the fears within me. I will keep trusting you until I see the promise realized in my life. In Jesus's name, amen.

Chapter Three

Settling for Less than God's Highest Priority

*"If we have found favor in your eyes," they said, "let this
land be given to your servants as our possession. Do not
make us cross the Jordan."*

Numbers 32:5

NUMBERS 32

To achieve God's priority for our lives, we must take initiative.
We can settle for less, or we can go for God's best. Several of
God's people discover this truth in this passage.

In the previous chapter, we studied a generation of Israelites
who failed to go in and take possession of the land God had promised them. So, rather than moving into the land, they wandered
in the desert for forty years, until everyone in that generation died
except Joshua and Caleb. Those men entered the promised land
because they were two spies who believed God's promise.

Now the next generation stands before the land their parents had been unwilling to enter. Numbers 32 gives the account of two and a half tribes of Israel: the Reubenites, Gadites, and the half tribe of Manasseh. God had promised all of Israel the land of Canaan, west of the Jordan River. But these two and a half tribes chose the land east of the Jordan, settling for less than God intended.

Settling for less is Satan's scheme to keep you from all God has for you. Satan wants to keep you in bondage so you can't go where God wants to take you. Let's look at some principles of settling for less, so you can be aware of the devil's schemes.

Settling for Less Finds Satisfaction in a Comfortable Christianity

> The Reubenites and Gadites, who had very large herds and flocks, saw that the lands of Jazer and Gilead were suitable for livestock. So they came to Moses and Eleazar the priest and to the leaders of the community, and said, "Ataroth, Dibon, Jazer, Nimrah, Heshbon, Elealeh, Sebam, Nebo and Beon—the land the Lord subdued before the people of Israel—are suitable for livestock, and your servants have livestock. If we have found favor in your eyes," they said, "let this land be given to your servants as our possession. Do not make us cross the Jordan." (Num. 32:1–5)

When we find satisfaction in a comfortable Christianity, we choose contentment and complacency over the promise.

This happened to the two and a half tribes. Satisfied with their location, they chose not to pursue the land God wanted to give them, even though the promised land was even better.

How many Christians and churches today choose a comfortable place in Christ? They treat the Word of God like a buffet, picking and choosing only the parts they like. They say, "I'll take all the grace of God I can get. Give me lots of God's love and big portions of his forgiveness. Sacrifice, commitment, service, and obedience—give me a little, but don't get carried away. Pastor, don't ask me for too much sacrifice or commitment, or I'll have to go to the church down the road. The gifts of the Spirit, the manifestation of the Spirit—no, I can live for Jesus without any of that. Besides, I don't believe they're for today."

The leaders of these two and a half tribes did not believe God had something better. In the same way, some Christians and churches see no need for the better things God has for them. They don't want the gifts and power of the Spirit to operate in their lives or services. They're content in their Christianity, satisfied in their apathy, or pleased with their powerlessness. Many are content with their relationship with Christ. Being content in Christ sounds spiritual, but we need a holy discontent over the comfortable and complacent state of our lives. God has much more "land" for us to possess in him.

These two and a half tribes chose to accept their present situation. Do you accept your present relationship with Christ? Or do you want more of his love, presence, power, grace, and intimacy? Have you accepted your present situation in life? Do you accept your disease, your bondage, your sin, your life as usual?

If that's you, maybe you need a holy discontentment. As we seek the Lord and draw closer to him, he places certain desires in our hearts, including a holy discontent for our present condition or situation. Ask the Lord to stir that restlessness within you for the things he wants to change.

One way you can assess your present contentment is by evaluating your pain point. Are you satisfied with where you are? Or do you want something more from God? What area of your life are you discontented with or maybe feel defeated in? Do you hunger for a closer relationship with God? Are you tired of living a casual Christian life? We can have peace in our hearts because of our relationship with the Lord, while at the same time, hunger for more. No matter where we are in our walk with the Lord, we should cry out for more of God. None of us have tapped into all his resources or experienced the depths of his love, grace, and power. God wants to take us to greater heights and deeper depths. Ask him to create a hunger in your heart for more of him and his presence, power, and nearness.

When we find satisfaction in a comfortable Christianity we fail to press through to God's promise.

Verse 5 is a significant statement: "Do not make us cross the Jordan." The Jordan River symbolizes a place of breakthrough. By crossing the river, the Israelites break through to God's promise. But the two and a half tribes were content to stay where they were rather than pressing through to God's promise.

If we want to get where God wants us to be, we must press through to God's promise. If your victory, healing, or miracle hasn't yet come, don't settle for less. In faith and prayer, press through. Keep believing God's promise for your life. Keep praying for a breakthrough into God's promise. Keep walking in faith and obedience until the promise becomes reality.

God has promised me some things in my ministry that I have yet to see, things I have been praying for and pressing toward for many years. I will continue to do so until I see evidence of those things in my life and ministry. In the words of the apostle Paul, "I do not consider myself yet to have taken hold of it, but one thing I do, forgetting what is behind and straining toward what is ahead, I press on toward the goal to win the prize for which God has called me heavenward in Christ Jesus" (Phil. 3:13–14).

God's promise to his church is the breakthrough of the Spirit found in Joel 2, where God promised to pour out his Spirit on all people in the last days. Peter referenced that prophecy to what just took place on the Day of Pentecost (Acts 2:16-21). There was the "sound like the blowing of a violent wind" and "tongues of fire that separated and came to rest on each of them" (Acts 2:2-3). The wind was a manifestation of the presence of the Holy Spirit. The fire was a manifestation of the power of the Spirit.

What began on the day of Pentecost didn't end there. We have yet to see the outpouring of the Spirit in our day. We have yet to see the working and moving of the Holy Spirit to the degree the early church did, on and following the day of Pentecost. We have yet to see the manifestation of the presence and power of the Spirit in signs, wonders, and miracles that they saw from this experience.

Not only was this a corporate experience by the group of people who were there when they heard the wind and saw the fire. It was also an individual experience when they each began speaking in tongues (a heavenly language God gives the believer). Peter spoke about this promise in his message: "This promise is for you, your children and for all who are far off—for all whom the Lord our God will call" (Acts 2:39). In other words, this promise of the Spirit is for you, the next generation, and every generation following.

Both John the Baptist and Jesus referred to this promise. John said, referring to Jesus, that "he will baptize you with the Holy Spirit and with fire" (Matt. 3:11). Jesus told his disciples to wait in Jerusalem for the Father's promise (Acts 1:4). Here we see the fulfillment of that promise, the baptism of the Holy Spirit. This experience continues through the book of Acts and throughout Paul's ministry.

In reference to the Holy Spirit, Jesus said, "Ask and it will be given to you; seek and you will find; knock and the door will be opened to you" (see Luke 11:9–13). He is speaking about the Holy Spirit. After his resurrection and before his ascension into heaven, Jesus told his disciples to "wait for the gift my Father promised," which was the baptism of the Holy Spirit (see Acts 1:4–5). In Luke 11, Jesus is not referring to the Holy Spirit's role in our salvation. He is referring to giving us a greater measure of the Holy Spirit, which is then demonstrated in the outpouring of the Holy Spirit in Acts 2, after the disciples had "joined together constantly in prayer," asking, seeking, and knocking (Acts 1:14).

I remember years ago when my kids were younger, we were having an outdoor BBQ at our house with some of our extended family. It was a hot summer's day. We didn't have any shade trees in our backyard, so I had to use the poles from our volleyball net to set up a tarp. Our plan was to set up the volleyball net so that we could play it at some time during the day. At one point, my son came up to me and asked if we could set up the net and play volleyball. I told him it was too hot and that we still needed the shade. Sometime later he came back and said, "Dad, *now* can we set up the net to play volleyball?" I gave him the same answer. He didn't let it go though. He came back a third time with more assertiveness and said, "Dad, you said that we could play volleyball." I thought later what a great example of asking, seeking, and knocking. The first time my Son just made a simple request. The second time he requested that we do it *now*. The third time he was holding me to my promise. Each time took on a greater level of tenacity. He was persistent. That's how God wants us to come to him concerning his promises. "Those who hunger and thirst for righteousness will be filled" (Matt. 5:6). God fills those who are hungry, hungry for those things that are *right* in his sight, hungry for him, hungry for his promises. It's no different when it comes to the fullness of the Holy Spirit. Jesus said to ask, seek, and knock.

When you receive the power of the Spirit, you have power to stand against the enemy, to live for Jesus, and to proclaim the good news of the gospel. This power will make a difference in your world. It enables you to love and live in new ways. God makes that power available to you. You can receive it because God is ready to give it to you.

A greater work of the Holy Spirit is available. If you want all God has for you, then ask him for the fullness of the Spirit and press through to God's promise of the baptism of the Holy Spirit.

For years, I have encouraged individuals and churches to pray through to a breakthrough. God is looking for hearts that desire a breakthrough. The prayer ministry is the church's greatest ministry because breakthrough won't come except through prayer. And yet the prayer ministry is the least attended and given the least attention. I challenge every church to pray through to a breakthrough. Pray through until you see a fresh move of the Holy Spirit in the life of your church. I challenge you personally as well. Pray through to a breakthrough, when you will see the evidence of God's promise of his power.

Praying through simply means to persist in prayer until the answer comes. "And will not God bring about justice for his chosen ones, who cry out to him day and night?" (Lk. 18:7). Day in and day out, seek God until you see the answer. Continue to bring that request before the Lord on a regular basis, asking, seeking, and knocking. When we do this, we not only seek an answer from the Lord, but we also seek the Lord himself, who will give you your breakthrough.

Settling for Less Prefers Comfort over Conquering

Moses said to the Gadites and Reubenites, "Shall your countrymen go to war while you sit here? Why do you discourage the Israelites from going over into the land the Lord has given them? This is what your fathers did when I sent them from Kadesh Barnea to look over the land. After they went up to the Valley of Eshcol and viewed the land, they discouraged the Israelites from entering the land the Lord had given them. The Lord's anger was aroused that day and he swore this oath: 'Because they have not followed me wholeheartedly, not one of the men twenty years old or more who came up out of Egypt will see the land I promised on oath to Abraham, Isaac and Jacob—not one except Caleb son of Jephunneh the Kenizzite and Joshua son of Nun, for they followed the Lord wholeheartedly.' The Lord's anger burned against Israel and he made them wander in the desert forty years, until the whole generation of those who had done evil in his sight was gone. "And here you are, a brood of sinners, standing in the place of your fathers and making the Lord even more angry with Israel. If you turn away from following him, he will again leave all this people in the desert, and you will be the cause of their destruction." (Num. 32:6–15)

When we prefer comfort over conquering, we fail to fight for God's best.

These two and a half tribes were unwilling to fight for the land God wanted to give them. Eventually they fought, but initially they refused. Remember, they said, "Do not make us cross the Jordan" (v. 6). They wanted to stay in their comfortable place instead of fighting to conquer the land.

We need to fight for the place God has for us, just as the Israelites did because that place is worth fighting for. If we neglect the fight, we can easily get comfortable and complacent.

To fight for what God wants to give us, we must engage in spiritual warfare. The enemy will fight to keep you from taking possession of God's promise. "For our struggle is not against flesh and blood, but against the rulers, against the authorities, against the powers of this dark world and against the spiritual forces of evil in the heavenly realms (Eph. 6:12). The enemy uses fiery darts of temptation, fear, discouragement, frustration, hopelessness, distraction, and sin to keep you out of the "land" God has for you. We must stand against the enemy in faith and prayer.

To stand against the enemy, we must take up the shield of faith, because a shield is a defensive weapon. Faith extinguishes all the flaming arrows of the evil one (Eph. 6:16). When faced with fear, discouragement, hopelessness, or any other "arrow" the enemy launches your way, stand in faith and believe in God's protection, provision, and promises.

We come against the enemy in prayer by taking the battle to the devil himself. While faith is a defensive weapon, prayer is an offensive weapon. Use the authority of the name of Jesus to send the devil running. Use prayer to press into Jesus in worship and thanksgiving. Prayer and praise break the enemy's strongholds. Prayer resulted in Peter's release from prison (Acts 12). Praise released Paul and Silas from their chains and opened the prison doors (Acts 16:25–26). Stand against the enemy in faith and come against the enemy in prayer.

When we prefer comfort over conquering, we fail to follow God wholeheartedly.

Verse 11 refers to the previous generation, who did not follow God's command to go in and take possession of the land: "Because they have not followed me wholeheartedly." Verse 12 refers to Joshua and Caleb: "They followed the Lord wholeheartedly."

Joshua and Caleb followed wholeheartedly. The previous generation did not. If we prefer comfort over conquering, we follow the example of the two and a half tribes, who failed to follow wholeheartedly.

To possess that "land," the place God has for us, we must follow the Lord in wholehearted obedience. If God calls us to do something as a church, we need to unite and obey so we can enter the place God has for us. The same is true for us personally. We must not fail to follow wholeheartedly. We can't pick and choose the areas in which we follow the Lord. If we do, we're not following him with all our heart.

Sometimes, following the Lord's leading doesn't make sense. It didn't make sense for me to leave a well-paying job or a fruitful ministry. However, following the Lord requires us to "trust in the Lord with all your heart and lean not on your own understanding; in all your ways acknowledge him, and he will direct your paths" (Prov. 3:5–6). It may not make sense to us, but God sees the big picture, and we don't. That's when trusting God comes into play. If we acknowledge him by seeking him in all our ways, asking him to direct our lives, he will direct us down the path he wants us to walk.

When we follow the Lord wholeheartedly, we follow him in wholehearted obedience, wholehearted faith, wholehearted trust, with our whole being. Even when it doesn't make sense, even when others disagree, even when it hurts.

Don't be deceived into thinking that as long as you don't turn away from the Lord, you're not settling for less. Not true. We can follow the Lord and still settle for less. The two and a half tribes didn't turn away from the Lord, but they still settled for less than God's promise. We can make the same mistake.

Settling for Less Compromises to Get Our Own Way

> Then they came up to him and said, "We would like to build pens here for our livestock and cities for our women and children. But we are ready to arm ourselves and go ahead of the Israelites until we have brought them to their place. Meanwhile our women and children will live in fortified cities, for protection from the inhabitants of the land. We will not return to our homes until every Israelite has received his inheritance. We will not receive any inheritance with them on the other side of the Jordan, because our inheritance has come to us on the east side of the Jordan." Then Moses said to them, "If you will do this—if you will arm yourselves before the Lord for battle, and if all of you will go armed over the Jordan before the Lord until he has driven his enemies out before him—then when the land is subdued before the Lord, you may return and be free from your obligation to the Lord and to Israel. And this land will be your possession before the Lord. (Num. 32:16–22)

When we compromise to get our own way, we build short of God's best.

This passage has the appearance of one conversation. But look at verse 16: "Then they came up to him." This is the beginning of a new conversation. The first conversation occurred when the two and a half tribes came to Moses and asked for the land east of the Jordan. They did not want to cross the river. Moses rebuked them, calling them a "brood of sinners." The tribes left after Moses rebuked them, and they went away to consider Moses's words. They discussed it and "then they came up to him" a second time (the new conversation). They came back to Moses with a compromise: they'd build pens for their livestock and cities for their families. Then they would fight alongside their countrymen and return after their fellow Israelites possessed their destination. They compromised so they could get what they wanted: the land east of the Jordan. They built short of God's best.

When we compromise to get what we want, we build short of God's best. That is the place we will possess.

As a church, do we build pens and cities? A church can have all kinds of successful ministries and programs, but without a breakthrough of the Spirit, we build short of our destination in Christ. If the working and moving of the Holy Spirit is not our priority, we build short of God's best. That does not mean those ministries are not important. They are, but they must take second place to the working and moving of God's Spirit in our churches.

Several years ago, after a time of prayer in the middle of the night, the Lord gave me a vision of the church. I saw a machine, hard at work with gears turning, steam pouring out—everything operating as it should. On a conveyor belt, lumps of clay moved into one side of this machine. Another conveyor belt transported vessels shaped like tall vases out of the other side. All the vases looked the same, flawless and in perfect condition.

Immediately following that vision, I saw a lump of clay on a potter's wheel. The wheel spun and someone's hands molded it into the same shape of the vessels on the conveyor belt. When the work was finished, I could not tell the difference between this vase and those on the belt. On the outside, they looked the same.

Then the Lord spoke to my heart. "The machine represents the church. The local church runs like a machine, with all its ministries and programs in place. But some of the vessels are manufactured, and others are made. The manufactured vases are missing the touch of the Potter's hand, the ministry of the Holy Spirit in the life of the church."

Without the ministry of the Holy Spirit, we merely manufacture disciples. But Jesus said to go and make disciples. Yes, the Holy Spirit is at work in the local church, but not to the measure God intends. We need to see a fresh move of the Holy Spirit in our lives and in our churches. We need to see a breakthrough of the Spirit. Without that breakthrough, we build short of God's best.

In the church, we've relied so much on everything other than the Spirit. The result has been doing God's will, man's way. King David did that when he attempted to move the ark of God back to Jerusalem. While moving the ark back to Jerusalem, "David and the whole house of Israel were celebrating with all their might before the Lord with songs and with harps, lyres, tambourines, sistrums and cymbals" (2 Sam. 6:5). They were having a worship service while the ark was being moved. Everything was going great until the oxen stumbled and a man named Uzzah reached out and took hold of the ark of God. God struck Uzzah down and he died because it was an irreverent act (2 Sam. 6:6, 7). It was God's will that they move the ark to Jerusalem, but David didn't use the Levites, who were the only ones designated by God to do so (1 Chron. 15:13). He was doing God's will, but man's way.

In the same way, we can be worshipping and serving God, all the while, doing God's will, our way. When we rely on our own creativity, ingenuity, programs, ministries, etc., rather than the work of the Holy Spirit, we are doing God's will, but man's way. We've been building God's church, short of God's best.

Yes, God uses all those things. But in the church, they've become our reliance. I do believe that methods can change as long as the message remains the same. I also believe the enemy has used that phrase in the church so that we will focus on the methods rather than the Spirit of God. Jesus is building his church and he uses us to build it. We can't afford to build short of God's best. Zechariah 4:6 says, "'Not by might nor by power, but by my Spirit,' says the Lord Almighty." It's not by our own creativity or ingenuity, programs or personality, but by the Spirit of God. It's by the Spirit that souls are saved, hearts are changed, lives are transformed, bodies are healed, bondages are broken and relationships are restored. In all that we do, let's rely on the Spirit to do what we can not do. We need a breakthrough of the Spirit in the church today.

When we compromise to get our own way, we settle for God's permission.

The two and a half tribes agreed to fight, which seems noble. But it was a compromise. Moses allowed the compromise, releasing them from their "obligation to the Lord and to Israel" (v. 22). God didn't send them out to wander in the desert, and he didn't annihilate the tribes. Moses permitted them this land because God permitted them the land.

God has two wills. He has a perfect will and a permissive will. These two and a half tribes had God's permission when Moses granted it to them, but they settled for God's permissive will rather than his perfect will. Likewise, we can choose God's permissive will. God says, "If that's what you want, you can have it." God will not force his perfect will on you. So be careful what you demand from God.

Imagine the church, all its ministries, and all its people traveling down the freeway on a bus. Each ministry is doing its part and carrying out its work. The men's ministry does what they do in the back of the bus. The women's ministry works in the middle, and the children's ministry has their thing going on in the front. Each ministry carries out its work and has its own functions, activities, and programs. But they don't realize the bus is in second gear, moseying down the freeway at twenty miles per hour, although it has the potential of going sixty and having greater influence.

Without a breakthrough and an outpouring of the Spirit, we operate in second gear, falling short of our potential. We can accomplish much more in the Spirit than we can on our own. But we can't run at our fullest potential until the power of the Spirit is released. The answer is not more functions or programs or ministries. The answer is a breakthrough of the Spirit.

Do you settle for less than God's best? Have you settled for infirmity in your body, accepting it as God's will? Have you given up and consider the bondage of sin and Satan as your lot in life? Don't settle for less. Pray through to a breakthrough.

Reflection

1. On a scale of one to ten, how strong is your hunger for God?
2. Identify an area of your life in which you have settled for less than God's best or have compromised to get what you want.
3. In what area of your life do you not follow the Lord wholeheartedly?
4. Has the Lord called you to do something that didn't make sense to your natural understanding? What was the outcome?
5. What steps can you take to seek the Lord in greater ways?

Encouragement: No matter what you've settled for in the past, you can get right back on the path to God's best. It's never too late to correct your course.

Challenge: Identify areas of your life that you would consider arrows the devil has been firing at you. Stand against him in faith and come against him in prayer. Tell another person who can stand with you in prayer and accountability.

Prayer: *Lord*, I ask your forgiveness for compromising to get my own way. Forgive me for settling for less than your best for me and not following you with all my heart. I'm ready now to do whatever you call me to do. I'm making you my priority in life and seeking you for your priority for my life. In Jesus's name, amen.

Chapter Four

Accessing God's Greater Portion

They said to Joshua, "The Lord has surely given the whole land into our hands; all the people are melting in fear because of us."
Joshua 2:24

JOSHUA 2

Life seldom hands us what we want on a silver platter. I know it hasn't for me. Most of us have to work, wait, pray, take steps of faith, and believe God for what he has for us.

From Numbers 32 to Joshua 2, we see the changing of the guard. Moses has died and Joshua is now in charge of leading the Israelites into the promised land. The Israelites have been living in a desert for forty years, and now they are about to enter a land flowing with milk and honey. The desert environment was not God's original plan.

How many of us as Christians fail to live in God's original plan for us? Rather, we serve the god of getting by instead of the God of greater measure. Do you need more love in a specific relationship? Do you need more peace in your home, more joy in your life? Or do you need more of God's presence and power in your life or more intimacy with Jesus? More than likely, we all do.

According to Ephesians 3:20, our God is a God of greater measure: "Now to him who is able to do immeasurably more than all we ask or imagine . . ." However, many Christians haven't accessed the greater measure God has for them.

God is able to do immeasurably more than all we ask or imagine, but he is not automatically and unconditionally obligated to do more. His ability gives us access to his promise. But how do we access God's greater portion?

> Then Joshua son of Nun secretly sent two spies from Shittim. "Go, look over the land," he said, "especially Jericho." So they went and entered the house of a prostitute named Rahab and stayed there. (Josh. 2:1)

Get a Vision of Greater Measure

To get a vision of greater measure for your life, begin by recognizing where you are.

Joshua told the two spies to go and look over the land. He wasn't asking them to develop a military strategy. God already had a plan of attack. Rather, he wanted them to get a vision for what God had for them. Remember, they had lived in a desert for the past forty years, and this generation had never had a glimpse of the promised land. The ones who had were dead and gone.

The spies left from Shittim because that is where they had camped. Shittim is another name for acacia, a large, thorny tree with rough, gnarled bark. It grew in desert climates. The Israelites were in a dry place, but that's not where they were to stay.

For us, this represents a place of spiritual dryness. Maybe that's where you are right now. Maybe you have no hunger or thirst for the Lord or the things of God. Maybe you don't pray regularly. Maybe Bible reading is hit and miss. And maybe that doesn't bother you.

We're in a dry place so we will develop hunger and thirst for the Lord and what he wants for our lives. There's nothing wrong with being in the desert. It's a good place to be, if it drives us to seek the Lord. But problems start when we become content in that place instead of seeking the Lord. We can grow in desert climates, but it's not God's ultimate plan for us to stay there. He sometimes puts us there to teach us something.

It's important to recognize where we are. Otherwise, we can't change. The best thing to do in your desert is to seek the Lord in greater measure.

I grew up in the church. I've been a Christian all my life, but I didn't seek the Lord in a greater measure until I was a young married adult. I had a Christian friend and coworker named Dave Ponsness. We grew in our walk with the Lord together. We became accountability partners without even planning it. During that season in my life, I grew stronger spiritually. Why? I recognized my spiritually dry state and decided to do something about it. Without Dave, I probably wouldn't have stuck with it and pursued God in a greater measure.

Recognizing our spiritual dryness should create a spiritual thirst for God and all he has for us. When we thirst, we seek God for a drink of his Spirit. David said in Psalm 63:1, "O God, you are my God, earnestly I seek you; my soul thirsts for you, my body longs for you, in a dry and weary land where there is no water."

David recognized his spiritually dry condition. This needs to be our heartfelt prayer as believers. It was my prayer back in the day, and still is today. You can make it yours as well.

To get a vision of greater measure for your life, also takes discovering where God wants you to be.

The text says the spies were sent from Shittim to Jericho. Shittim was where they presently were, but Jericho was where they were going.

Joshua told the two spies to investigate Jericho. Jericho was called the City of Palms because it was an oasis—a place of fertile ground in a desert. Acacia trees grew in a place of dryness. Palm trees grew in an oasis. When we find ourselves in a place of spiritual dryness, we should look to God for a spiritual oasis. God wants to take us to a place of refreshment in him.

That spiritual oasis is a place of abundance in Christ and fullness in the Holy Spirit. There we find a greater measure of God's resources. Many Christians live in spiritual poverty. But God has an abundance of love, forgiveness, grace, blessings, gifts, power and provision stored up for us. God's storehouse of greater measure has all those things and more.

Ask God to give you a vision of greater measure for the life that he has planned for you. If there is one thing that I've learned, it's that God's vision for me has grown and taken on greater detail over the past thirty years. God has continued to reveal more and more to me concerning his plans for my life, and he will do the same for you.

Take Steps of Greater Measure

The promised land was unknown territory for this generation. The spies sent into the land forty years earlier are now dead. This time, only two spies went in. They went to look over the land and check out the area they were to conquer. They tested the water, so to speak, and discovered that the people melted in fear of them. During this test, God confirmed to them that they were to go in.

Taking steps of greater measure requires testing unknown territory.

To access God's greater measure, we need to step into unknown territory. There comes a time when you need to go, you need to take a step, you just need to do something.

You may be at a time in your life when you need to step into unknown territory. It's unknown because you haven't been there before. You're taking on a new role, greater responsibility, or a change in your life. It will stretch and grow you.

If you need a job, begin testing unknown territory by knocking on employers' doors and applying for positions. When I needed a job shortly after graduating high school, I applied at different companies, but one in particular I checked back day after day for several weeks until I finally got an interview and was hired. Is God calling you to leave your position, job, or even community and step into unknown territory? Whatever your need, take prayerful and practical steps toward that which God has for you.

When I took a position at Suncrest Family Worship Center in Nine Mile Falls, we began to think about moving to that area so we could be part of the community and build relationships. The church was across town from our home, in a different county. However, moving to that community meant I had to drive in the opposite direction to get to work every day. Since this pastorate was a volunteer position, I decided to look for a job closer to the church. I found one in a perfect location. So I left my job of fifteen years (the one out of high school), and started working for a young company. Three weeks into the job, they decided I wasn't the person they were looking for. They didn't expect to have to train me for the position, so they let me go. Here I was, without a job. I didn't know what to do.

Before long, my previous manager heard what had happened and asked me to come back. It wasn't what I'd hoped for, but I took him up on his offer. Did I make a mistake by leaving? Did I fail to hear from the Lord? Was that a step of foolishness rather than faith?

The Lord quickly made it clear to me that he was testing my faith to see if I would leave my secure position to follow his lead. One year later, our company was bought out and my entire department was laid off. It was then I was asked to go on staff at the church, and my family and I moved into that community.

Sometimes practical steps can be scary and risky, but God will always honor your step of faith. He's got your back. He will work things out for your good, even if you miss his will and blow it. If I could do it over again, would I make the same decision? Absolutely.

While taking steps of greater measure, you will also need to trust God completely.

Forget, for just a moment, whose house the two spies hid in. Instead, think about this: when they took steps of obedience, a door opened for them. The Bible doesn't give us all the details. We know they went to Jericho and entered a house. How did that happen? Did they go door to door? Did they meet this woman on the streets of the city, and did she invite them to her home? How did they come across this woman without the whole town finding out who they were and what they were doing (although they were eventually found out)? How did they know she wouldn't turn them in?

We don't know everything that took place, but we know God divinely directed their steps. He met them there and opened a door for them.

When we step into unknown territory, we must trust God from

there. We don't know what the future holds, but God will work out the details. We need only to be obedient, and God will take care of the things we cannot take care of ourselves.

I worked at a computer company for sixteen years (the same company in my earlier story). During those years, the Lord called me to the ministry. I knew I needed to begin my biblical studies, but I needed to understand the Lord's timing. I prayed and asked God whether this was the time to step out and enroll in Bible college. Through my friend Dave, the Lord revealed that he couldn't direct my steps if I wasn't walking. So I moved forward with my studies while working a fulltime job, working in the ministry, and raising a family.

Many times we wait for God's leading before we take a step. Sometimes that's God's will. And sometimes we need to start walking. Then the Lord can either close or open doors, according to his will. I'm glad I tested unknown territory at that time. Early on, I knew it was the right move.

When I was pastoring my first church, I wanted to purchase a certain facility to use as our church building. The price was much more than we could afford. But I knew that, if God was in it, money wouldn't be an issue. So we had a fundraising campaign and raised just over $100,000. It was a large amount, especially for a small church, and maybe just enough for a down payment for this building. We made an offer, and the owner was in the process of accepting when a bigger offer came in. We could not counter, which was a disappointment.

Days later, a vacant piece of land went up for sale for just under $100,000. We voted to purchase it instead. We ended up with almost nine acres, paid in full.

If we had not tested the unknown territory, we wouldn't have raised the money to purchase that land. The Lord closed one door but opened another. But we had to take practical steps and test the unknown territory before we could see God's intervention.

So without getting ahead of God, we need to take practical steps. He will either open or close doors, according to his perfect will, as we test unknown territory while trusting him completely.

Invest in Greater Measure in Another's Life

Experiencing more to this life isn't just about us. It's also about helping others find faith in Christ or helping them grow in Christ so they can access God's greater portion.

One of the ways we can make a greater investment in the lives of others is by loving them unconditionally.

When the spies entered Rahab's house, they walked into her life as well, despite her sin. These men could have reasoned their way out of going to a prostitute's house. But God had great plans for Rahab. Because of her faith, God fulfilled those plans. Matthew 1:5 puts Rahab in the lineage of Jesus. This woman made a huge contribution to humankind: Jesus was one of her offspring.

It is possible to hate the sin but love the sinner. You might wonder how reaching lost people and ministering to growing Christians can help you access God's greater measure. Jesus gives the answer in Matthew 6:33: "Seek first his kingdom and his righteousness, and all these things will be given to you as well." As we seek first God's kingdom, he will provide for us. As we bless others, God blesses us.

Consider Job's story. After he prayed for his friends, God blessed him with twice as much as he had before. Job accessed God's greater measure.

Who is the Lord asking you to help? Who is the one person you already identified earlier to reach out to? Cultivate that relationship in greater ways.

We can also invest in another's life by seeing them through to victory.

We accomplish that by refusing to give up on them, even when we don't see any good coming from our investment in them. The spies didn't merely enter Rahab's house. They stayed there (Josh. 2:1). They entered a lost person's life and stayed with her, swearing an oath to see her through to victory and to salvation. Likewise, we see people through to victory or salvation by interceding for them in prayer and ministering to them in a loving, personal way.

Invest your life in another person. Stay with them by praying for them regularly and building a relationship. Take a personal interest in them. The Lord will open a door for you to share your faith with them or strengthen them in theirs.

Years ago I wanted to buy a hunting pistol. It wasn't just a matter of going out and buying it, though. I had to save up the money for it, which took close to a year. When I had saved up enough money, I bought it. But since I didn't have a concealed-weapons permit, I couldn't take the gun home. Instead, I had to wait a week for my background check to clear. My name was on the gun. I had the receipt telling me it was mine. But I didn't possess it until the waiting period was over. But once I possessed the gun, it was mine to use, and I got a nice buck with it. This wasn't just any buck. It was the biggest buck I have ever taken.

Likewise, there's a greater measure of God's power, presence, blessings, and gifting waiting for you. God's already purchased and provided them for you. Your name is on them, you just need to take possession of them as you access God's greater portion for your life.

Reflection

1. Where do you envision yourself ten years from now? Is this where you want to be?
2. What hope, promise, desire, or vision has God given you?
3. What steps of greater measure can you take to draw nearer to the place God is leading you?
4. How can you invest in a greater measure in someone else's life?

Encouragement: We all have regrets, but I've never regretted taking a step of faith into new territory, even if it didn't turn out the way I thought it would. However, if I hadn't taken those steps, I would have regretted the missed opportunity, wondering how it might have turned out.

Challenge: If you have sought the Lord's direction, asking him if you should take a certain step, but haven't received an answer, perhaps the Lord is waiting for you to make a move. I didn't have a clear word from the Lord before I left my job, but since a door opened for me, I walked through it. God ultimately had it all under control.

Prayer: *Lord*, I want to access your greater portion. Help me to discern when you are calling me to take a step of faith into unknown territory and when you want me to wait. Also, show me whose life I can invest in and how I can do that, loving them unconditionally as you love me. I trust you completely. In Jesus's name, amen.

Chapter Five

Breaking Through to God's Planned Promotion

*Then you will know which way to go, since you have
never been this way before.*
Joshua 3:4

JOSHUA 3

Promotions are always an exciting experience. When we move up to a better position in our careers, when we move into another house that better meets our family's needs, when we experience relief from a chronic health issue, when your church grows numerically, whenever we move into something better than where we were or what we had before; we could classify those as promotions in our lives. Sometimes, things we would consider demotions are not necessarily so. Sometimes God has us take one step back to take two steps forward.

When I took my first church in Liberty Lake, Washington,

that was my experience. Things started out well, but before too long, I had to make some tough decisions that put me in a difficult position. One in particular, I had to let a staff member go, which I didn't want to do. He and his wife were great assets to the church and our leadership team. I loved them dearly. But for reasons I'm not going to go into, I knew I had to make a tough call. In doing so, half the church left. One of the truths that the Lord taught me through that experience was that sometimes God adds by subtraction. Sometimes, we have to take a step backward before we can move forward. We needed to take a step backward numerically before we could move forward spiritually.

When I ran into this staff member sometime later, he thanked me for letting him go because he was in a position in another church that was a good fit for him. Now, he is pastoring his own church.

We all have an area in our lives where we need God's divine intervention. I know I did at that time in the life of our church. We need God to heal or deliver or restore or to intervene in some area of our life. It might be physical, financial, emotional, relational, or any number of things. That intervention is called a breakthrough. What is it for you? God has a breakthrough planned for your promotion.

Wait at the Place of Breakthrough and Listen for God's Instructions

> Early in the morning Joshua and all the Israelites set out from Shittim and went to the Jordan, where they camped before crossing over. After three days the officers went throughout the camp, giving orders to the people: "When you see the ark of the covenant of the Lord your God, and the priests, who are Levites, car-

rying it, you are to move out from your positions and follow it." (Josh. 3:1-3)

The Jordan River represents a place of breakthrough for the Israelites. Once they crossed the Jordan River, they would enter the place God had for them. This was the closest they had come to the promised land in forty years.

In verse 1 the Israelites left Shittim, where they were, and camped at the Jordan before crossing over. Why did they have to wait? Because they needed God's instructions. In Joshua 1:11, God told Joshua when and where to cross the river: "Three days from now you will cross the Jordan here." Three days, right here. But they did not know how to cross the flooded Jordan since the waters were too high. They were to camp and await God's instruction while the spies enter the land and hide from their pursuers for three days.

You may be at the place of breakthrough. You are at the Jordan River, so to speak. As you've prepared for God's promotion by following his leading in your life, you've moved into position. Now you sit at the place where you must listen for God's instruction. What does he want you to do next?

Wait at the Place of Breakthrough and Move at God's Direction

After the three days, God instructed the people to move in the direction He would lead them. The ark of the covenant was symbolic of God's presence, and their instructions were simple: follow God's lead by following the ark.

I know I'm not the only one who sometimes wants to help God out and get things moving. But when we do that, we move ahead of God instead of following him. This is when we need godly patience. This may be a short time or, as with me, it could be a long

wait. Listen for God's instructions and then move in God's direction. Although we often want to take matters into our own hands
after we sense God's leading, we must resist the temptation. God's
timing is vital.

This describes my ministry life. I've had to listen for God's instruction and then move in his direction every time he led me to
leave one ministry for another. Even when I knew he would soon
move me on, I had to wait for his direction. I did not move forward
until I had a clear word from the Lord.

When I resigned from Suncrest Family Worship Center in
Nine Mile Falls, the Lord spoke to me about a specific move. This
was the church I spoke of earlier—the one the Lord had told me I
would someday pastor. This was the second time we ministered at
Suncrest Family Worship Center. The first time I was a children's
pastor, then youth and associate pastor. Now here I was the lead
pastor, living in God's promise of pastoring this church, but God
was calling me to step down. So I did. It didn't make sense at the
time, just as it hadn't made sense when I resigned from my first
church. God had called me to and promised me this church, but
nonetheless, this was a word from the Lord.

One of the several ways the Lord spoke to me about that move
was 1 Chronicles 4:39–40: "They went to the outskirts of Gedor
to the east of the valley in search of pasture for their flocks. They
found rich, good pasture, and the land was spacious, peaceful and
quiet. Some Hamites had lived there formerly."

When I read these two verses, the Lord spoke clearly to me:
"You are going to move east of the valley where you had lived formerly." The east side of the Spokane Valley is Liberty Lake, where
we lived before moving back to Nine Mile Falls. Liberty Lake is
literally "east of the valley" where we had lived "formerly." If that
wasn't enough, the Lord confirmed the move with the sale of our

house. When the Lord spoke that verse to me, I wrote the date next to the verse in the margin of my Bible: May 29, 2007. The confirmation came the day we closed on our next house. I had forgotten about that Scripture until the day we signed. I looked up the verse in 1 Chronicles, and to my amazement, we were signing the papers on our house, the exact day that I had written next to that verse. The Lord had fulfilled his promise exactly one year after he gave it: May 29, 2008. One year to the very day, we lived east of the valley where we had lived formerly.

Prepare Yourself for a Breakthrough by Separating Yourself from the World

> Then Joshua told the people, "Consecrate yourselves, for tomorrow the Lord will do amazing things among you." (Josh. 3:5)

Before we can have a breakthrough, we must prepare ourselves. This preparation always involves consecration: the act of setting ourselves apart for God's use. God calls his people to consecrate themselves because something is about to happen, and we'll need to set ourselves apart to be prepared to carry out God's will.

In Exodus 19:10–11, the Lord said to Moses, "Go to the people and consecrate them today and tomorrow. Have them wash their clothes and be ready by the third day, because on that day the Lord will come down on Mount Sinai in the sight of all the people." The washing of their clothes symbolized inner cleansing. The Israelites needed this because God was going to come down in the sight of all the people. They had to get cleaned up because they were about to meet with God.

In Joel 2, one of God's stipulations for the outpouring of his Spirit is the consecrating of the assembly, the purifying of all the people. "Even now," declares the Lord, "return to me with all your heart . . . consecrate the assembly . . . and afterward, I will pour out my Spirit on all people" (Joel 2:12, 28). The purpose of consecration is to prepare ourselves for what God wants to do next in our lives.

In 2 Corinthians 7:1, Paul says, "Let us purify ourselves from everything that contaminates body and spirit, perfecting holiness out of reverence for God." We are called to "cleanse ourselves" in order to be "prepared to do any good work" (2 Tim. 2:21). We know that when we confess our sins that God purifies us (1 Jn. 1:9), but like we see here, we are also called to purify ourselves, to cleanse ourselves from those things that would contaminate our body and spirit. Consecration is essential for our preparation in kingdom work.

How is God calling you to consecrate yourself? What does he command you to separate yourself from? Could it be what you view on the television? Could it be sites you visit on the internet? Maybe an unhealthy relationship needs to end. Maybe he wants you to give up something good in greater consecration to the Lord. Only you can answer that. Make it a matter of prayer, and see what God lays upon your heart.

It's time for each of us to search our souls, to separate ourselves from things that contaminate our body and spirit. We need to put away the idols that claim more of our affection and attention than God does. Confess those things to God and turn away from them. "Throw off everything that hinders and the sin that so easily entangles" (Heb. 12:1). It's time to get cleaned up and get ready to be used of God.

This cleansing isn't about salvation. When a person comes to faith in Christ and is born again, they come as they are. God will clean them up. When we consecrate ourselves, we're preparing for our next step. We can't take that step while carrying the baggage of the world or holding onto sin. That is why we need to "throw off everything that hinders and the sin that so easily entangles." Those things keep us from moving into the place God is calling us in Christ.

If you were scheduled to meet with the president of the United States because he had plans to use you as his representative on a special assignment, you probably wouldn't show up sweaty and stinky after working in the yard all day. You are still a citizen of the United States however you look (or smell), but you would get cleaned up and dress appropriately. It's the same way spiritually. We need to be cleansed of our sin by confessing those sins to God and turning from them to move into that which God has for us.

Prepare Yourself for a Breakthrough by Dedicating Yourself to the Lord

Joshua told the people to consecrate themselves because the next day God would do amazing things among them. If we want to see God act powerfully, we must separate ourselves from the world in dedication to the Lord.

I want to see God move in a powerful way in my life and in the lives of his people, but first, we must turn away from anything that would hinder us from experiencing God's power. To do that, we don't have to be perfect. We can't. But sin isn't allowed in God's presence, so it must be removed. Only the priest could enter the holy of holies, where the glory of God came down, and only after his own sins were atoned for. As "priests" of God, we know Jesus has paid for our sins, but "without holiness, no one will see the Lord" (Heb. 12:14). Jesus said, "Blessed are the pure in heart, for they will see God" (Matt. 5:8).

In separating ourselves from the world, we must dedicate ourselves in greater ways to the Lord. Christianity is not a matter of how close we can live to the world with God's permission, but how far we are willing to separate ourselves from the world in dedication of our lives to God. We should never live as close to the world as we think we can. Rather, we should separate ourselves from the world, dedicating our lives to God. There are Christians who live as close to the line as possible. They believe as long as they have God's permission, all is well. They don't realize God is calling them to a life of separation. Sanctification is the practice of separating ourselves from the world, denying ourselves the sinful desires of our heart, and dedicating our lives in greater measure to the Lord. When we come to Christ, we are made holy, clothed in the righteousness of Jesus Christ. But in everyday living, our practice must line up with our position. That's where spiritual growth takes place. In one respect, we are made holy, we are sanctified, but in another, we are being made holy, we are being sanctified.

Some things are not a matter of sin, but of separation. We sometimes permit ourselves to do certain things that are not sinful, but they may be a matter of separation. Just because it's not a sin doesn't mean we should do it. God might call us to separate ourselves from a certain practice.

Take drinking, for example. For me, drinking is a sin because "Everything that does not come from faith is sin (Rom. 14:23) and I couldn't do it with a clear conscience. You may not feel the same way. Regardless of whether it is a sin for you or not, it is a matter of separation. I don't condemn people nor cast judgment on them for drinking, and it doesn't bother me to be around people who drink. Although, I've never seen anything good come from it either. Alcohol destroys lives and relationships. It's addictive and destructive. It doesn't add any value to life. On the contrary, it only steals, kills, and destroys lives and relationships. My wife and I have set the example of choosing not to drink, and we hope our children will pass this conviction on to their children. What you decide is between you and God.

The Lord may call you to separate yourself from good things. What if he called you to give up coffee for a month or to give up your social media or your hobby for a season? When God was about to descend on Mount Sinai in sight of all the people, He told Moses to consecrate the people and to "abstain from sexual relations" as a part of their consecration (Ex. 19:10, 11, 15). For some people, that might be easier to give up than coffee.

Whenever the Lord asks you to separate yourself, he's preparing you for a breakthrough.

Crossing at the Point of Breakthrough Acts on God's Word

> Now the Jordan is at flood stage all during harvest. Yet as soon as the priests who carried the ark reached the Jordan and their feet touched the water's edge, the water from upstream stopped flowing. It piled up in a heap a great distance away. (Josh. 3:15–16)

In Joshua 3:8, God told Joshua to tell the priests, "When you reach the edge of the Jordan's waters, go and stand in the river." Here we see when "their feet touched the water's edge, the water from upstream stopped flowing."

The priests could have stood on the riverbank all day and night, and nothing would have happened. The water didn't stop flowing until they stepped into the water. The point of breakthrough came when they acted on God's word.

The same thing happened when Moses and all the Israelites stood at the Red Sea, and Pharaoh's army closed in. God told Moses to lift his staff and raise his hands over the water. When Moses did, the water parted, but Moses had to act on God's word to see the breakthrough take place. (Ex. 14:15, 21–22).

You may be camped at the place of breakthrough, listening for God's instructions. When he gives it, act on it, and you will experience a breakthrough.

Every time God called me to resign a ministry position, he first spoke to my heart, showing me a change was coming, and I would soon leave. But I didn't act until he said, "Now is the time."

Crossing at the Point of Breakthrough Steps into New Territory

> The priests who carried the ark of the covenant of the Lord stood firm on dry ground in the middle of the Jordan, while all Israel passed by until the whole nation had completed the crossing on dry ground. (Josh. 3:17)

When the Israelites acted on God's word, stepping into the water's edge, he performed a miracle. The water piled up a great distance away, and they crossed over on dry ground, stepping into territory they had never been before.

When we act on God's word, he will promote us to a new level, to new territory. That new territory might be miraculously healing your marriage or your body. That new territory might be your deliverance from bondage. Like the Israelites, that new territory may be a place you have never seen before to do what you've never done before. But if you listen for God's instructions, move at his direction, and act on his word, he will promote you to the place he has for you.

We might not receive this promotion the moment we act on God's word. It may come at a later day, or it may be instant.

When I resigned from my last church, acting according to

God's word, he did not release me from the position for several months. I thought I'd leave within a few weeks. God wanted me to stay for a few months. When I resigned, the church asked me to stay until they found a new pastor. I agreed, and the transition was smooth for me, my family, and the church.

One Sunday, when my wife and I visited the church I had previously pastored, the current pastor, Bart Orth, asked me to pray after the worship time. I agreed, planning to walk up to the platform after the last song and lead the congregation in prayer. But during worship, the Lord told me to call people forward to receive prayer. So I did.

After the service, a lady told me she had felt compelled to come to this church, even though she usually attended somewhere else. The Lord had told her there would be an altar call, and if she went forward, he would heal her. She'd battled pneumonia the past six weeks, her antibiotics giving her no relief. When I gave the altar call, she came forward, and the Lord healed her. God could have healed her right where she stood during worship, but he wanted her to take a step of faith. When she acted on God's word, he responded to her faith and obedience and healed her. In the one case, it took several months. In the other, it was instantaneous.

God has a promotion planned for your life. That promotion will take you into new territory. By following these basic principles, "you will know which way to go since you have never been this way before."

Reflection

1. In what area of your life can you further consecrate yourself to the Lord? Do you need to separate yourself from something that hinders your walk with the Lord?

2. Has the Lord given you an instruction, but you have not followed through?
3. What next step do you need to take to move in God's direction?
4. Who could hold you accountable to follow through with the next step?

Encouragement: A breakthrough is coming for you, no matter how long you've waited or how discouraged you feel. It could be just around the corner. Don't give up now.

Challenge: Ask the Lord for clear instructions to move toward the promotion he has planned. Does he want you to get involved in a ministry? Does he want you to reach out to someone? Wait for God's instruction and move at his direction.

Prayer: *Heavenly Father,* I want the new territory you have for me. Show me what that new territory represents. Help me to be sensitive to your instructions so I can move according to your directions. In Jesus's name, amen.

Chapter Six

Experiencing God's Ordained Purpose

*The manna stopped the day after they ate this food from
the land . . . that year they ate of the produce of Canaan.*
Joshua 5:12

JOSHUA 5:1–12

As Christians, we have yet to experience the measure of life that Jesus came to give us. We've become comfortable with where we are spiritually. We're content with living beneath the abundant life God intended for us. We don't experience the gifts, life, love, peace, power, or presence he has for us.

I want God's people to break through into the life God has for them. This often means we go where we've not gone before in Christ, to do what we've not done before in the Spirit.

That's why I like the book of Joshua. It represents God's people experiencing breakthrough. For the Israelites, the promised land is no longer a hope, a prayer, or something to look forward to in the future. It's a present reality.

When we've had a breakthrough, God's purpose for us will no longer be a dream, but reality. When you break through, a fourfold purpose results.

God Will Demonstrate His Power in You

> Now when all the Amorite kings west of the Jordan and all the Canaanite kings along the coast heard how the Lord had dried up the Jordan before the Israelites until we had crossed over, their hearts melted and they no longer had the courage to face the Israelites. (Josh. 5:1)

When God demonstrates his power in you, he will cause your enemy to be overcome by you.

Because they heard about the Israelites' miraculous crossing of the Jordan, the kings of the enemy nations no longer had courage to face them. Their hearts melted in fear because they knew they were done. They knew they were defeated before a single battle started—even before they could see it.

We know that Satan is our enemy, and we are at war against him and his kingdom. But we each have another enemy to overcome, another giant to conquer. Our enemy has been causing havoc, and as a result, we fear and doubt and live in defeat. The giant might be uncontrolled anger, pornography, addiction, spiritual apathy, complacency, lust, or greed, just to name a few. But God will demonstrate his power in you, causing you to overcome instead of being overcome.

To overcome your enemy, you need to take the offensive, to launch an attack, to declare war on your enemy and the powers behind it.

The Israelites didn't merely set up camp and wait for the enemy to attack. Instead, Israel launched the attack. We take the offensive by exercising our authority over our enemy in prayer, telling bondage, addiction, and ailment to flee in Jesus's name. Like Jesus, we can use the sword of the Spirit, which is the Word of God, against the devil himself (Matt. 4:1–11; Eph. 6:17). By God's power, he will enable you to conquer your giant.

God Will Make an Extreme Change in You

> At that time the Lord said to Joshua, "Make flint knives and circumcise the Israelites again." So Joshua made flint knives and circumcised the Israelites at Gibeath Haaraloth. (Josh. 5:2–3)

God will make an extreme change in you because he's planning a greater work for you.

Circumcision was a covenant, or agreement, between God and his people, Abraham's descendants: "I will establish my covenant as an everlasting covenant between me and you and your descendants after you for the generations to come, to be your God and the God of your descendants after you" (Gen. 17:7). Circumcision was the agreement God made with Abraham. The Lord would be their God, and they would be his people.

The men who left Egypt were circumcised, but the next generation, born in the desert, was not. So God reestablished his covenant with this new generation. Circumcision was an extreme change in these men's lives. But they needed it because God had planned a greater work for them: driving out the enemy and taking possession of the land.

The New Testament shows us God no longer requires circumcision in the flesh as a covenant between himself and his people. In both Testaments, he refers to circumcision as concerning the heart, by the Spirit (Rom. 2:29).

What is circumcision of the heart? Deuteronomy 30:6 tells us. "The Lord your God will circumcise your hearts and the hearts of your descendants, so that you may love him with all your heart and with all your soul, and live." Circumcision of the heart refers to the "cutting away" of sin from our lives. That takes place when Jesus comes into our lives and takes away all the sins of our past and gives us a new heart inclined toward him. He no longer counts our sins against us. He makes our hearts new. This means we have turned our backs on a life of sin. We may occasionally sin, but we no longer live a life of sin, and it no longer has control over us. When we sin, we repent. We confess it to the Lord and walk away from it.

When God plans a greater work for us, he needs to make a greater change in us. As he does, we should place our focus on being rather than doing. Being comes before doing. Character comes before responsibility. The greater the responsibility, the greater the character needed. A person of great character can be trusted with great responsibility. This extreme change comes with a breakthrough.

Jesus said we will do what he has done and even greater things (Jn. 14:12). God is calling you to do greater things in his name. These greater things come when we simply seek Him. As I grew in my relationship with Jesus, drawing closer to him, he birthed in me a vision for greater things. You can ask God what those greater things represent for you. But don't seek the greater things of God as much as you seek the God of greater things. As you seek him, he will show you the greater things he is calling you to, and he'll put a desire in your heart for them. Delight yourself in the Lord, and he will give you the desires of your heart (Ps. 37:4). He puts those desires in your heart as you delight yourself in Him. Make

Jesus your heart's delight, and he will give you your heart's desire. We do that through our expression of prayer, praise, worship, and thanksgiving.

God Will Remove the Disgrace of Your Past from You

> Then the Lord said to Joshua, "Today I have rolled away the reproach of Egypt from you." So the place has been called Gilgal to this day. (Josh. 5:9)

When God removes the disgrace of your past from you, he will give you a new identity.

To reproach means to disgrace or shame. Egypt represents the Israelites' past bondage—the time they were slaves in Egypt. They were slaves to their past bondage, so God promises to roll away or remove their shame and disgrace of bondage. They will no longer be known as slaves.

When God gives a new identity to you, your past will no longer define you. You will no longer be known by the sins and bondage of your past. You will be known as a man or woman of God because his work will be evident in your life.

After you've experienced a breakthrough, you will no longer be known by the stigma attached to your name. People will see you and know you as the person you have become through God's work in your life.

You will no longer be known as a liar, drug addict, grouch, worrier, adulterer, or fearful person. God will remove the old name and give you a new identity.

Your part is to walk out that new identity. You can't go back to the way you were. When God delivers a person from their past, they must walk in the light of their new identity. At times, the devil will try to trip you up. He wants you to return to the way you were. He will place temptations in front of you, trying to drag you back to your old way of living, back to your bondage. But when Jesus sets you free you are free indeed (Jn. 8:36). That means you can now live in freedom without fear of returning to your old way of life.

Jesus gives you the ability to walk and live in freedom, but you still must choose to walk in obedience to him.

God Will Make a New Provision for You

> The day after the Passover, that very day, they ate some of the produce of the land: unleavened bread and roasted grain. The manna stopped the day after they ate this food from the land; there was no longer any manna for the Israelites, but that year they ate of the produce of Canaan. (Josh. 5:11–12)

When God makes a new provision for you, he will no longer supply you with your former resources.

When the Israelites began to eat the produce of the land, the manna was gone. They ate manna during their forty years in the desert. It was like a wafer or flake that appeared on the ground. God provided manna for the Israelites each morning, and they gathered it six days a week. But after they entered the land, they ate the produce of the land. The manna was gone.

When you've experienced a breakthrough, you no longer live on past resources. If your past resource has been a pill to meet your physical or emotional needs, you no longer have to rely on it as a source of help, because God has healed you. If your past resource has left you broke and bankrupt, God wants to bring new provision. If your past resource hasn't met the needs of your family, your marriage, or your children, God will give you new provision.

This new provision is the healing and delivering power of the Spirit. It will be new resources from heaven.

Continue to seek God for the personal breakthrough that you need in your life because when that breakthrough comes God will demonstrate his power in you, make an extreme change in you, remove the disgrace of your past from you, and make a new provision for you.

Reflection

1. Which of these four results of a breakthrough inspires you the most? Why?
2. In what area of your life do you want to see a breakthrough?
3. What old provision would you like to get rid of? What new provision would you like to see God bring?
4. What changes has God already made in your life? What additional changes would you like to see him make?

Encouragement: God has a purpose for you. He will accomplish these four truths in your life. You don't need to work for them. Rather, you will simply walk them out.

Challenge: Continue to seek and trust the Lord to work out his perfect purpose in your life. Don't look back, and don't let your past define you. God is calling you forward in Him.

Prayer: *I love you, Lord,* for all you mean to me. I want to thank you in advance for fulfilling your purpose in my life. Help me to continue to follow you and to draw close to you daily. I'm excited to see what you are going to do in and through me in the days to come. In Jesus's name, amen.

Chapter Seven

Exercising God's Unlimited Power

And he ordered the people, "Advance! March around the city, with an armed guard going ahead of the ark of the Lord."

Joshua 6:7

JOSHUA 5:13–6:27

The theme of the book of Joshua is possessing the promised land. In the first few chapters, Israel prepares to cross the Jordan, and then they enter the land. But they still need to possess it.

This is the Israelites' first battle. God planned for them to possess the land of Canaan, but they couldn't as long as their enemy occupied it. So they had to remove the enemy.

But Jericho was tightly shut up, a wall surrounding the city. The Israelites had no way of getting to the enemy. The wall stood between them and God's promise.

In this passage, we'll see what it took for the Israelites to conquer Jericho and begin to occupy the promised land (even though they were not to occupy Jericho). In this chapter, we'll look at exercising God's power so you can occupy the "place" God has for you in Christ.

Expect God's Intervention

> Now when Joshua was near Jericho, he looked up and saw a man standing in front of him with a drawn sword in his hand. Joshua went up to him and asked, "Are you for us or for our enemies?" "Neither," he replied, "but as commander of the army of the Lord I have now come." Then Joshua fell facedown to the ground in reverence, and asked him, "What message does my Lord have for his servant?" The commander of the Lord's army replied, "Take off your sandals, for the place where you are standing is holy." And Joshua did so." (Josh. 5:13–15)

We can expect God's intervention when we get on God's side.

After Joshua basically asks, "Whose side are you on"? The man standing before Joshua says "neither," but lets him know who he is: the commander of the army of the Lord. He's establishing he's on God's side. After Joshua understands, he falls face down in reverence, humbling himself before God and saying, "What message does my Lord have for his servant?" Joshua humbled himself in service to God.

Many people want God to be on their side, but God calls us to be on his side. We want him to come to us on our terms, but he calls us to come to him on his terms. It's not a matter of living for ourselves and getting God on board with us. It's living our lives for Christ and getting on board with him. He has a place for us, a new life for us. He has a position for us to fill in his kingdom. But we must come to him on his terms: in surrender to him as his servant.

Some people come to Christ on their own terms. They want the fire insurance without the premium. They want salvation without the service. They cast their vote for Jesus rather than surrendering their lives to Him. There is a difference between true and false conversion, true and false disciples. Jesus said, "Not everyone who says to me 'Lord, Lord,' will enter the kingdom of heaven, but only he who does the will of my Father who is in heaven" (Matt. 7:21). True disciples surrender their lives to Christ, following him in faith and obedience.

On the outside, we can appear to people as righteous, but on the inside be full of hypocrisy and wickedness (Matt. 23:28). We can go through the motions. We can go to church and even write a check, but still not be in a right relationship with Jesus. Like the Israelites, we can even worship the Lord and still serve our idols (2 Kgs. 17:41). An idol is anything that takes the place of Jesus in your life. Who or what gets your attention and affection in the place of Jesus? A lot of things and people need our attention and affection, and rightly so, but Jesus must be our priority. Anything can become an idol. Jesus must be the center of our lives.

Getting on God's side also includes removing everything that separates us from him.

Joshua had to remove his sandals because the place he was standing was holy. It's the same command given to Moses at the burning bush (Ex. 3:5). Because of God's presence, the ground they stood on was holy. They had to remove everything that came between them and God, just as we must do today.

We naturally pick up wrong attitudes, practices, habits, and thoughts from the world. We need to remove those that are unholy,

so we can remain in direct contact with our holy God. This is repentance. When we come to Christ in repentance, we confess and
forsake our sins. We turn our backs on sin and our faces toward
God. We purify ourselves from everything that contaminates body
and spirit, perfecting holiness out of reverence for God (2 Cor. 7:1)
by removing those unholy practices from our lives.

You can't love the world and God at the same time. You can't
hang onto the world with one hand and God with the other. Repentance is turning completely away from those things that hinder
our relationship with Jesus. David said, "Search me, O God, and
know my heart; test me and know my anxious thoughts. See if
there is any offensive way in me, and lead me in the way everlasting" (Ps. 139:23–24). If we approach God in humility and genu-
inely ask Him to search our hearts and show us any offensive way
between us, He will do so. Then we must confess and turn away
from that which comes between us and God.

Trust God's Contribution

> Now Jericho was tightly shut up because of the Israel-
> ites. No one went out and no one came in. Then the
> Lord said to Joshua, "See, I have delivered Jericho into
> your hands, along with its king and its fighting men."
> (Josh. 6:1–2)

When we're fighting to possess our promised land, God con-
tributes by working in the spiritual realm.

Verse 1 tells us Jericho was tightly shut up. In other words,
it was impenetrable in the natural realm, but not in the spiritual
realm. In verse 2, the commander of the army of the Lord says to
Joshua, "I have delivered Jericho into your hands." He doesn't say,
"I'm going to deliver" or "I am delivering." He wasn't speaking in

the future or even in the present, but in the past. It's a done deal. He already fought and won the battle in the spirit.

When Joshua looks up, he sees the commander of the army of the Lord standing in front of him, a drawn sword in his hand. Why did he have his sword in his hand instead of its scabbard? He didn't draw it to use it on Joshua. Rather, if God's army of angels had just come from doing battle in the spiritual realm, defeating every power of darkness over Jericho, then he has just come from that battle with the sword still in his hand. That is why, when Joshua asks whose side he is on, the angel replies, "Neither." He just came victoriously from battle and says, "See?" as if showing Joshua what he and God's army accomplished. That's why he could say he wasn't on either side. His job was already done.

Before you see God's promise fulfilled in your life, before you see the answer to your prayer, before you see a breakthrough, the battle must first be fought, and the victory won in the heavenlies.

The enemy lives behind that wall. We can't see him, but we can see the wall he erected. The wall is not the problem. The problem is the enemy behind the wall. The world has ways of bringing down the walls. But if we don't deal with the enemy, he will erect another wall because we dealt with the symptom, but not the problem. A psychologist or modern medicine might help you bring down your wall, but if you don't deal with the enemy who erected the wall, he'll build another.

When God's contribution is completed in the spiritual realm, we see the effect in the natural realm.

Victory had been won in the spiritual realm, but Israel didn't see it in the natural realm for seven days. The Israelites hadn't conquered Jericho yet, even though the battle was already fought and won in the spirit. After the battle has been won in the spirit realm, we can then take the land.

Although it might look as if God is not doing anything about your need, your prayer, or his promise, he is. He's working behind the wall, in the spirit realm, because the battle must first be fought and won there.

Follow God's Instructions

> When the trumpets sounded, the people shouted, and at the sound of the trumpet, when the people gave a loud shout, the wall collapsed; so every man charged straight in, and they took the city. (Josh. 6:20)

When we follow God's instructions, we can expect the walls in our lives to fall.

God gave the Israelites explicit instructions at different times in their journey. They had to follow these instructions to see God work on their behalf, and this time is no different. They marched around the city once a day for six days, sounding trumpets. Then on the seventh day, they marched around the city seven times. After the seventh time, they sounded the trumpets and shouted. When they fulfilled God's instructions, the wall collapsed.

If you want walls to collapse in your life, you must fulfill your marching orders, even if they seem strange or don't make sense. The Israelites must have thought God's instructions were a little "out there." Yet they moved forward in faith and obeyed the word of the Lord, and so must we.

When we follow God's instructions, we can expect victory.

Once the wall came down, the Israelites went in and gained the victory. They didn't bring down the wall. God responded to their obedience and brought down the wall.

We have walls as well. Those walls represent the things between us and God's promise—things that keep us from the abundance and fullness God has for us. It might be a wall of disease, poverty, addiction, contention in your home, rebellion in your teenager, or strife in your marriage. You will not have victory until that wall comes down, but God will bring it down if you follow his instructions by walking in obedience to him and doing what he calls you to do. His instructions might seem crazy. The Israelites probably felt that way for marching around a wall for seven days and shouting to bring it down. But they followed God's instructions, the wall fell, and they gained the victory.

Reflection

1. After careful self-evaluation, would you say you get on God's side, or do you try to get God on your side?
2. What evidence led you to that conclusion?
3. What changes do you need to make to get on God's side?
4. What instructions is God giving you?

Encouragement: No matter how sinful your life has been or is today, God can forgive you and release you from your past. "Let us then approach the throne of grace with confidence, so that we may receive mercy and find grace to help us in our time of need" (Heb. 4:16). You can approach God and receive mercy and forgiveness.

Challenge: Don't automatically decide something is not from the Lord just because it doesn't make sense to you or seems strange. God may be calling you to something that doesn't make sense in the natural.

Prayer: *Lord*, I humble myself before you. Please show me my heart as you see it. Show me if you see anything offensive that I need to correct. It's my heart's desire to live a holy life that pleases you. Help me to do my part so walls will come down in my life. Here are the walls I want to fall. (Name those walls.) In Jesus's name, amen.

Chapter Eight

Defaulting on God's Greatest Potential

*Israel has sinned; they have violated my covenant, which I
commanded them to keep.*

Joshua 7:11

JOSHUA 7

When the Israelites conquered Jericho, God commanded them not to take any of the people's belongings for themselves. All the silver and gold, along with items of bronze and iron, were to be put in the treasury of the Lord. But during the conquest, Achan took silver, gold, and a robe and hid them in his tent. This wasn't a casual, "I screwed up" sin. This was a sin of defiance and rebellion. Achan had a clear word from God, but he willingly and spitefully defied that command.

The next place to conquer was Ai. After spying out the land, the Israelites determined they didn't need as many soldiers to take the city, since it was much smaller than Jericho. But in their attack, the men of Ai chased Israel away, and about thirty-six men were killed. The hearts of the Israelites melted. The Lord speaks to Joshua and says, "Here's why: there is sin in the camp." God said, "Israel has sinned" (v. 11).

Because of one man's sin, the entire Israelite community suffered. Achan's sin of rebellion became the sin of Israel. That sin was the obstacle to conquering any more land. If they hadn't taken care of that sin, the Israelites would have defaulted on the land God had promised them. The promise was conditional upon their faith and obedience.

Sin will cause us to default on the potential God has given us, and it will keep us from experiencing abundant life.

The Obstacle of Sin

> But the Israelites acted unfaithfully in regard to the devoted things; Achan son of Carmi, the son of Zimri, the son of Zerah, of the tribe of Judah, took some of them. So the Lord's anger burned against Israel. (Josh. 7:1)

The Obstacle of Sin Forfeits God's Peace

Because of one man's sin, the Lord's anger burned against the entire community of Israel.

We hear all the time about God's love and mercy and grace, and rightly so. But the sin of rebellion angers God. When anger is present, peace is absent. You've experienced that in your home. If only one of you gets angry, peace is gone. Likewise, sin in the church will drive out the peace of God. And when a nation sins, it forfeits God's peace.

Show me a family in which one member is in sin, and I will

show you a family that is not at peace. There may be peace in certain relationships in that home, but perfect peace as a whole family unit is gone. The whole family suffers because of one individual's sin. Why? Because sin brings suffering.

Look at our own nation, and you'll see that is true. Our country has willingly rebelled against God. As a result, our nation no longer experiences peace. Our borders have been invaded by terrorists. The crime rate just among our youth has risen 600 percent since 1962, when prayer was removed from our schools. The United States has some of the world's highest rates in violent crime, divorce, teenage pregnancies, voluntary abortions, and illegal drug use. God has lifted his protecting hand from our nation, and we have forfeited his peace. We kicked God out of our nation, our schools, and our government, and we murder the unborn, and we wonder why we have the problems we do. Likewise, when individuals persist in a life of sin, they are not at peace with God, because the sin of rebellion forfeits God's peace.

But if we love and obey God, we experience peace with him. This peace fills your life, regardless of your circumstances. God wants to bestow peace upon your life, your marriage, your family, and your relationships.

The Obstacle of Sin Forfeits God's Power

> Israel has sinned; they have violated my covenant, which I commanded them to keep. They have taken some of the devoted things; they have stolen, they have lied, they have put them with their own possessions. That is why the Israelites cannot stand against their enemies; they turn their backs and run because they have been made liable to destruction. (Josh. 7:11–12)

The presence of sin results in the absence of God's power.

Due to Achan's sin, God's power was not available to fight for Israel. In the same way, we can't stand against the enemy, and we live powerless lives. We move from one powerless relationship to another. We open our lives to Satan's attacks and influence because God's protecting power is no longer present to restrain him. We live enslaved to that sin because Satan holds us in bondage to it.

God's power, on the other hand, is available to us as we live in a right relationship with him. Then we can go to the Lord for strength to fight our battles. We can access his help anywhere, any time. Therefore, we don't need to depend upon our own strength, wisdom, or abilities to get through a challenge or crisis.

God stands by to help us, but he waits for us to ask. Isaiah 31:1 says, "Woe to those who go down to Egypt for help, who rely on horses, who trust in the multitude of their chariots and in the great strength of their horsemen, but do not look to the Holy One of Israel, or seek help from the Lord." How often do we rely on other resources rather than seeking help from the Lord? He wants us to rely on him. You never have to wonder whether you are bothering him with your many requests. He delights in helping you. Call upon him in the day of trouble (Ps. 50:15). Call upon him in the moment of crisis. Most importantly, call upon him before you face trouble or crisis. Maintain daily communion with him in prayer, not just when you need him to fix something.

The Obstacle of Sin Forfeits God's Presence

In the second part of verse 12, God tells Israel, "I will not be with you anymore unless you destroy whatever among you is devoted to destruction." He told Joshua, "My presence will no longer be with you unless you deal with the sin."

God wants us to live in his presence. In the presence of the Lord is fullness of joy and a sensitivity to the leading and promptings of the Spirit. His glory dwells there, and it's where he manifests himself.

But when we live in rebellion, we forfeit God's presence. It doesn't matter how much we've experienced his presence in the past; if we allow sin to rule our lives, we forfeit God's presence. I am not suggesting God will leave you or forsake you. We know he will never leave us nor forsake us, but we will not see the manifest presence of God operating in our lives if we willingly hold on to our sin.

The manifest presence and power of God are tangible, and they take our faith to new levels. It's inspiring and encouraging to see God at work in even the smallest details.

The Removal of Sin

> Then Joshua said to Achan, "My son, give glory to the Lord, the God of Israel, and give him the praise. Tell me what you have done; do not hide it from me." (Josh. 7:19)

The Removal of Sin Exposes the Sin

We begin the process of removing the sin by exposing the sin. In verse 19 Joshua asks Achan to expose the sin. "Give it up. Tell me what you did."

Achan's sin was exposed, but he didn't confess until it was exposed. God exposed his sin. We can expose our own sin, or God or someone else can do it. I would much rather expose my sin to the Lord before he exposes my sin to me. He already knows about it, but we must agree with God and acknowledge our sin to him.

We also need God to expose our unknown sin to us so we can turn from it. We need to see sin in a new light. Godly sorrow leads us to repentance (2 Cor. 7:10). This godly sorrow forces us to make changes. Worldly sorrow merely makes us sorry we got caught. But the conviction of the Holy Spirit leads us to godly sorrow and true repentance.

The Removal of Sin Confesses the Sin

> Achan replied, "It is true! I have sinned against the Lord, the God of Israel. This is what I have done: When I saw in the plunder a beautiful robe from Babylonia, two hundred shekels of silver and a wedge of gold weighing fifty shekels, I coveted them and took them. They are hidden in the ground inside my tent, with the silver underneath." (Josh. 7:20–21)

It's one thing to expose the sin or to have it exposed to us, but it's another to confess, "It is sin. I was wrong. Forgive me." Even though Achan confesses his sin, he and his family still suffered the consequences. Sin has consequences, even when we confess and ask for forgiveness. If a murderer comes to faith in Christ, Jesus will forgive him, but the murderer will still face a prison sentence or the death penalty. Even though God will forgive your unfaithfulness to your spouse when you repent, you still may end up getting a divorce. Yes, accept God's forgiveness and forgive yourself, but accept the consequences of your sin. God can still bring good to your life and out of your life.

First John 1:9 tells us, "If we confess our sins, He is faithful and just and will forgive us our sins and purify us from all unrighteousness." The first person we need to go to with our sin is Jesus, confessing it to him and asking for his forgiveness. You might also need to confess to someone else. James 5:16 says, "Confess your sins to each other and pray for each other so that you may be healed." When we have wronged someone, we need to confess to them, ask for forgiveness, and take responsibility for our actions. Don't sidestep it or minimize it or make excuses. Just lay it out there and take the blame. The other person may or may not accept your apology, but you did what you needed to do.

The Removal of Sin Forsakes the Sin

> Then Joshua, together with all Israel, took Achan son of Zerah, the silver, the robe, the gold wedge, his sons and daughters, his cattle, donkeys and sheep, his tent and all that he had, to the Valley of Achor. Joshua said, "Why have you brought this trouble on us? The Lord will bring trouble on you today. Then all Israel stoned him, and after they had stoned the rest, they burned them." (Josh. 7:24–25)

Confessing sin is only the first step to repentance. When we have confessed our sin, we must forsake our sin. True confession doesn't continue in the sin. We must also forsake it. That means we remove it from our lives and make restitution. If we've done wrong, we need to make it right. If we're doing something illegal, we need to stop. If we're at odds with someone, it's time to remove the contention and find healing and forgiveness in the relationship. When sin is dealt with, like the Israelites, you will be back on track to experiencing more to life in Christ. If you do not, you will default on God's greatest potential for your life.

Reflection

1. Ask God to reveal any sin in your life that you may not previously have considered sin.
2. Confess the sin to God and someone else, if necessary.
3. What steps will you take to forsake the sin God revealed to you?
4. Think back to the last time you experienced God's hand at work in your life in a tangible way.

Encouragement: There is no sin God can't forgive. After you have confessed and forsaken your sin, accept God's forgiveness by forgiving yourself. The devil loves to keep reminding you of it so you will beat yourself up over it, but it's in the past. Continue to look to the Lord for healing, but always remember you've been forgiven.

Challenge: If, after you've confessed your sin to God, you need to ask someone's forgiveness, go to that person and tell them, "I was wrong. Please forgive me."

Prayer: *Thank you, Heavenly Father*, that I can approach your throne of grace with confidence, knowing you will be merciful to me as I confess my sin. Please forgive me for (name a known sin in your life). Please search my heart and expose any sin I am not aware of. Help me to see my sin as you see it. Thank you for having mercy on me and forgiving me. In Jesus's name, amen.

Chapter Nine

Moving Forward in God's Perfect Plans

Peter . . . described how the Lord had brought him out of
prison . . . and then he left for another place.
Acts 12:17

ACTS 12

Most of us would like to make a change in our lives, but maybe don't have the means to do so. The change you desire might require an education, finances, gifts, talents, abilities, or experience you don't have. The change might be financial, physical, relational, emotional, or occupational. You might feel like a prisoner to your job, your struggling marriage, depression or anxiety, sickness, or addiction. You might think there's no way out.

Peter was in that place. He'd been arrested, thrown into prison, and chained between two guards. He could do nothing to change his circumstances. Naturally speaking, he had no way out. God had a plan for his life: carrying the gospel message. But Peter was going nowhere.

Moving forward with God's plans for your life is possible when God intervenes, but also requires action on your part.

Acquire Divine Motivation

> It was about this time that King Herod arrested some who belonged to the church, intending to persecute them. He had James, the brother of John, put to death with the sword. When he saw that this pleased the Jews, he proceeded to seize Peter also. This happened during the Feast of Unleavened Bread. After arresting him, he put him in prison, handing him over to be guarded by four squads of four soldiers each. Herod intended to bring him out for public trial after the Passover. So Peter was kept in prison, but the church was earnestly praying to God for him.
>
> The night before Herod was to bring him to trial, Peter was sleeping between two soldiers, bound with two chains, and sentries stood guard at the entrance. Suddenly an angel of the Lord appeared and a light shone in the cell. He struck Peter on the side and woke him up. "Quick, get up!" he said, and the chains fell off Peter's wrists. (Acts 12:1–7)

Acquiring divine motivation begins with prayer.

By the time of Peter's arrest, Stephen had already been stoned to death. James had just been put to death by the sword. Now Peter awaits trial the next day. Herod will decide his fate, and he had just put James to death. Even knowing that, Peter slept.

Having that knowledge, I would be thinking if God didn't spare

James's life, he probably won't spare mine. I would not be asleep. I would be praying my heart out for the Lord to spare my life.

Why did Peter sleep? Did he have peace about the possibility of dying? Did the Lord give him a personal word that he would get him out of there? We don't know. But Peter's friends were not okay with this. They prayed while Peter slept.

I wonder what Peter's fate would have been if others had not prayed. God limits himself to the prayers of his people, so our prayers matter. He wants his people to seek him. If God's will is done on earth as it is in heaven, regardless of our prayers, Jesus would not have taught us to pray, "Thy will be done on earth as it is in heaven" (Matt. 6:10). If God's will were done on earth as it is in heaven without our prayers, the world wouldn't be in a mess. The determination of man in prayerfulness always precedes the intervention of God in the miraculous. In other words, our determined prayers always precede God's intervention.

Deliverance requires prayer. Sometimes, like Peter, we need divine motivation. For Peter, the motivation was an angelic visitation. For us it might be a gentle nudge from the Holy Spirit. Or, like Peter, it might require something more drastic to awaken us.

Once we have the motivation for a change, God will instill in us a sense of urgency.

Notice what the angel didn't do. He didn't tap Peter on the shoulder or shake him gently, whispering "Peter, wake up." No, he struck him on the side. I don't know if the angel kicked him or what, but this was no gentle awakening.

Peter was supernaturally motivated when the angel appeared, striking him on his side, waking him up, and telling him, "Quick, get up!" Why quick? What was the hurry? Did they have to make a quick getaway before the soldiers woke up? No, God had already taken care of them. The angel struck Peter to instill in him a sense of urgency of what God was about to do in his life. The first thing was to free him from prison.

Most of us probably won't experience an angelic visitation, so how will God divinely motivate us? Like Peter, it may come as an answer to prayer. It will certainly evolve from prayer. God will supernaturally motivate you and instill a sense of urgency in you as you pray. God may motivate you through his Word or another person speaking into your life. It may even come through a crisis. God is not limited to how he will motivate us and instill in us a sense of urgency.

Take Necessary Action

> Then the angel said to him, "Put on your clothes and sandals." And Peter did so. "Wrap your cloak around you and follow me," the angel told him. Peter followed him out of the prison, but he had no idea that what the angel was doing was really happening; he thought he was seeing a vision. (Acts 12:8–9)

Take necessary action by preparing to move away from your present situation.

The second thing the angel told Peter was to put on his clothes and sandals and wrap his cloak around him. It was up to Peter to prepare to move away from his present situation.

How do you prepare to make a move if you don't know how to free yourself, where you are going, or what God is calling you to? When you pray, the Lord will place on your heart the things you need to do. As he motivates you through prayer, he will also show you the things you should leave behind.

While I was working in a management position at Cabela's,

an outdoor recreation store, the Lord first began stirring my heart about moving on. I had been at the Post Falls, Idaho, store (just across the Washington and Idaho border) for almost four years at the time. It was then I began to prepare for a move. I knocked on doors to see where God was leading me. I applied for a position in a new Cabela's store in Union Gap, Washington. I began mentoring someone in my department to take over my management position. I sent out letters to churches, requesting speaking engagements, not even knowing if that was ultimately where God was leading me. I also applied for a lead pastor position at a church in Spokane, where I lived. I had no idea what God had next for me. The door that opened was a promotion in the new store in Union Gap, located in central Washington. So my wife and I moved away from our family, including our son and daughter and their families, our extended family and friends, to live in a different city and start in a new management position at the first Cabela's Outpost.

If you are hungry to be released from the present and move into the future God has for you, begin asking God about a change he would like to make in your life and how to prepare for that move. God will open or close doors, according to his will for your life.

Taking necessary action will then require an uncalculated risk.

Acts 12:9 tells us Peter followed the angel out of the prison. It wasn't enough for Peter to get himself dressed and prepare to move. He had to act, had to follow the angel out of the prison.

Consider the risk Peter took. His life already hanging in the balance, he had to get past four squadrons of four soldiers each. That's sixteen soldiers. Had Peter gotten caught, he would have sealed his fate. But he didn't weigh his options or calculate the consequences.

Sometimes following the Lord's leading in our lives requires an uncalculated risk. It's uncalculated because it doesn't make sense. It's unreasonable. It's illogical. For Peter, it defied the laws of nature. Nobody had ever done this before.

In another uncalculated risk, Peter stepped out of the boat to walk on water (Matt. 14:22–33). This was not a nice sunny day with water as calm as glass. Peter didn't sit on the edge of the boat and dangle his feet in the water to see if it would support his weight. No, it was stormy and dark, and the wind blew up white-caps. Stepping out of the boat was unreasonable, illogical, and life threatening.

After our preparations, there comes a time to move. Sometimes God's leading goes against all logic. But like Peter, if you don't take the step, you won't get the miracle. All the other disciples stayed in the boat because that was logical, but only Peter experienced the miracle. And in jail, Peter took a risk to move in the miraculous because he knew Jesus was with him. He will be with you as well.

Twice, when I resigned from my church, I knew it was the Lord's leading, even though I did not have another job or ministry to go to. I had no way to pay my bills or take care of my family. I had no clue what God would do. I stepped into uncertainty. Yet, the Lord saw me and my family through every time. Through the years, he has always led us to the exact place he'd planned for us.

Follow Through to Completion

They passed the first and second guards and came to the iron gate leading to the city. It opened for them by itself, and they went through it. When they had walked the length of one street, suddenly the angel left him. Then Peter came to himself and said, "Now I know without a doubt that the Lord has sent his angel and rescued me from Herod's clutches and from everything the Jewish people were anticipating." When this had dawned on him, he went to the house of Mary the mother of John, also called Mark, where many people had gathered and were praying. Peter knocked at the outer entrance, and a servant girl named Rhoda came to answer the door. When she recognized Peter's voice, she was so overjoyed she ran back without opening it and exclaimed, "Peter is at the door!"

"You're out of your mind," they told her. When she kept insisting that it was so, they said, "It must be his angel."

But Peter kept on knocking, and when they opened the door and saw him, they were astonished. Peter motioned with his hand for them to be quiet and described how the Lord had brought him out of prison. "Tell James and the brothers about this," he said, and then he left for another place. (Acts 12:10–17)

When we've followed through to completion, we'll see evidence of our release.

That release doesn't always take place right away. Notice the progression. They passed the first and second guards. They went through an iron gate that opened by itself and then they walked the length of a street. God could have transported Peter out of prison the same way he transported Philip from the desert to Azotus after he baptized the Ethiopian (Acts 8). But Peter had a step-by-step deliverance. God supernaturally intervened by keeping the guards asleep and opening the gate for him.

Verse 11 tells us that Peter came to himself. Until then, he thought he was seeing a vision rather than reality. Like Peter, we will encounter obstacles and impossibilities. But God will work supernaturally until he releases you from the present to move you into the future. There are things that God is doing right now that you can't even see taking place. There are things that the Lord is doing behind the scenes that won't be manifested until your release comes.

Moses told the Israelites that God had sent him to free them from their bondage. But plague after plague and judgment after judgment had to take place before the Israelites could see evidence of their release. Things got worse for them after Moses came to free them, but ultimately their release was manifested when they finally walked out of Egypt (Ex. 4:18–12:42).

When God brings release to that area of your life, he may then lead you in an unintended direction.

Acts 12:17 tells us that, after Peter appeared to the people who prayed for him, he "left for another place." If he hadn't, Herod would have found him and probably would have executed him for escaping prison. The following verses tell us Herod made a careful search for Peter but did not find him. So Peter probably left the city and maybe even Herod's jurisdiction of Judea. We don't know where Peter went. He's not mentioned again until chapter 15 and he's back in Jerusalem. Herod had died, so the threat on Peter's life had passed.

It's safe to say that, wherever Peter was before Herod's death, he was in the place where God led him. Maybe he didn't even know where he was going when he left Jerusalem. I believe God used Peter's imprisonment to lead him where he wanted him to be. Who knows, maybe Peter would not have left Judea any other way.

As with Peter, God has a place for each of us that may include detours to bring us to our destination. He usually sends us down an unexpected path to our future. When you continue to follow through to completion, God moves you in the direction he intended for you even though it was unintended by you.

God has new territory for you. That territory may be a place of health and healing after an extended illness. It might be a different line of work or job position, a call into the ministry, or a new location for your family. Only God knows what new territory he has for you until he reveals it to you.

After resigning the pastorate over twelve years ago and beginning my ministry as an evangelist, I was forced to get a job. What I didn't realize at the time was that God called me to be an evangelist in the workplace for a season. I also didn't realize I was walking into my own personal prison. I wanted to preach the gospel as I had done before, but for now that was on hold.

The Lord had a purpose for Paul and Silas's imprisonment. After their chains fell off and the prison doors miraculously opened, Paul led the warden and his family to Christ (Acts 16:16–34). Was it God's will for Paul to stay in jail? Not at this time. But God had him in prison, literally and figuratively, so Paul could reach others for Jesus.

Even though God blessed me in my secular work, I wanted to preach the gospel, because that's what God called me to do. And in his timing, he will open that door for me again.

Notice it was when the church prayed for Peter, that the "chains fell off Peter's wrists." Peter did nothing to bring it about. Peter still had to walk out his deliverance, but he couldn't go anywhere while the chains kept him bound. The church prayed in faith, the chains fell off, and Peter was free.

Like Peter, we need God to release us from something before he can release us to move into his plan for us. When he released the Israelites from Egypt, the land of bondage, they moved toward the land flowing with milk and honey.

We all need God to free us from the things that keep us from moving forward. Peter was set free from his chains. The Israelites were set free from Egypt when they crossed the Red Sea. The Red Sea represented an obstacle to their freedom. When they crossed it, they broke free from the land of slavery. Until then, they were still enslaved to their past.

Both deliverances required an act of faith. Peter stepped out in faith by walking out his deliverance. The Israelites walked through the Red Sea when Moses acted in faith, parting the waters.

Prayer can break the chains that bind you. You don't have to work for your deliverance. You don't have to measure up to a certain standard. God wants to break the bondage of sin and Satan in your life. Exercise your faith until you break free. This might require one more prayer. Or, as with Moses, it might take a simple act of faith. Don't give up now. When the chains come loose, when the waters part, walk out your deliverance into the future God has for you.

Reflection

1. What do you feel imprisoned to?
2. Are you desperate to break free, or have you resigned yourself to living with it?
3. How do you presently pray for deliverance? How do you ask others to pray for you?
4. Could God be leading you in a direction you've never considered?
5. What steps can you take to move from where you are to where God wants you to be?

Encouragement: If you're in a place you do not want to be, remember that God has you there for a reason and for a season. Thank the Lord for allowing you to be there for now and ask him to teach you what you need to learn and use you to reach those around you.

Challenge: Make the most of this opportunity to learn, grow, and reach others for Christ. God will use the skills you are learning now for your future.

Prayer: *Lord*, please break the chains that hold me in bondage. Let me feel your presence and peace, and please confirm to me that I am free from my bondage. Let the chains fall. In Jesus's name, amen.

Chapter Ten

Pursuing God's Driving Passion

As long as it is day,
we must do the work of him who sent me.
John 9:4

JOHN 9

Jesus had a specific work that his Father sent him to do. Toward the end of his life he prayed, "I have brought you glory on earth by completing the work you gave me to do." (Jn. 17:4).

When Jesus was twelve years old, he went with his parents to Jerusalem for the Feast of the Passover. But when his family, along with other relatives and acquaintances, started for home, Jesus stayed behind. When his parents discovered he was missing, they went back to Jerusalem and found him in the temple courts, listening to the teachers and asking them questions. Jesus said, "Didn't you know I must be about my Father's business?" (Lk. 2:49 KJV).

Being about his Father's business was to do the work he was sent to do.

Just as we have certain tasks and responsibilities associated with our daily work, we also have work to carry out in the kingdom of God. After all, "we are God's workmanship, created in Christ Jesus to do good works, which God prepared in advance for us to do" (Eph. 2:10). What is the work he calls us to? We all have something different to contribute to the kingdom of God depending upon God's call on our lives along with the gifts, talents, and abilities God has given us. There is one work, however, that we all share and are called to that I want to address here. It's important that we identify that work so that we can be about our Father's business as well.

Our Call to the Father's Work

> As he went along, he saw a man blind from birth. His disciples asked him, "Rabbi, who sinned, this man or his parents, that he was born blind?"
>
> "Neither this man nor his parents sinned," said Jesus, "but this happened so that the work of God might be displayed in his life. As long as it is day, we must do the work of him who sent me. Night is coming, when no one can work. While I am in the world, I am the light of the world." (Jn. 9:1–5)

Our call is to reach unbelievers.

God's passion is people. He rescues them from the clutches of the devil and from spending eternity separated from him. To pursue God's driving passion as a way of life we must first understand our call to that work.

Our call to the Father's work is to reach unbelievers while there is still time. We must do the work of the Father because soon it will be too late, and we will no longer be able to work. That work is reaching the lost. Jesus said, "I have come to seek and save the lost" (Lk. 19:10). He ultimately accomplished that by dying on the cross for the sins of mankind. But long before that, he was still about the work of the Father.

Our call is commissioned by Jesus.

While Jesus was in the world, he was the light of the world (v.5). But what happened when he left this world, rising again to return to the Father? In Matthew 5:14 and 16, Jesus said, "You are the light of the world" and to "let your light shine." And in John 20:21, he said, "As the Father has sent me, I am sending you."

Jesus said, "You are the light of the world. And since you are the light of the world, let your light shine before men. As my Father sent me, I am sending you." This shows us that Jesus passed the assignment to us.

Our Contribution to the Father's Work

> Having said this, he spit on the ground, made some mud with the saliva, and put it on the man's eyes. "Go," he told him, "wash in the Pool of Siloam"(this word means "Sent"). So the man went and washed, and came home seeing. (Jn. 9:6–7)

We fulfill our contribution to the Father's work through meeting a need by natural means.

To understand the passage, we need to make note of three seemingly insignificant words in verse 6: "Having said this . . ." Those three words make a connection between Jesus's words and what he is about to do. First, he said we must do the work of the one who sent him, and then he demonstrated the work by making mud from dirt and saliva and applying it to the man's eyes.

Why did Jesus do that instead of merely touching the man's eyes or speaking healing to him as he did for blind Bartimaeus (Mk. 10:46-52)? I don't believe this was just about a man's healing. Remember, Jesus is teaching his disciples about the "work" the Father has sent him to do. Now Jesus defines a principle about that work: Reaching unbelievers begins with ministering to their personal needs through natural means. He took natural elements like saliva and dirt to make mud and put it on the man's eyes, meeting a need by natural means. He could have used supernatural means alone, but he didn't.

I remember singing the song "This Little Light of Mine" as a child growing up in church. I never knew exactly what it meant other than living a good life for others to see. But in Matthew 5:16 Jesus tells us to let our light shine before men so they may see our good deeds and praise our Father in heaven. We let our light shine by our good deeds, but not just by living a good life before others, also by doing good to and for them.

However, being always comes before doing. God is more concerned with who we are than what we do, but that doesn't negate the importance of doing. Acts 10:38 tells us Jesus went around doing good. Likewise, we let our light shine by doing good to people.

We can find many ways to meet the needs of others by natural means. We can help others with a project or chore around their house. Or we can help with home repairs, prepare a meal, pray for them, or simply be a friend. Befriending a person can be the first step in ministering to them. Look for ways to build friendships within your sphere of influence and minister to people's needs, no matter how small or insignificant it may seem.

Supernatural intervention will then follow our contribution.

When this man washed the mud off his eyes, he could see. The saliva and dirt didn't give this man his sight. If that were the case, we would have the cure for blindness. Rather, the supernatural intervention of God, combined with this man's faith and obedience, made him see. Remember, Jesus is teaching his disciples and us how to do the kingdom work he calls us to do.

Results come when God adds his supernatural element to your efforts. He does that by softening the person's heart toward him, convicting them of their sin, and revealing himself to that person through you. This can lead to the salvation of their soul. Reaching unbelievers begins with meeting their personal needs through natural means, bringing supernatural intervention.

Making a Connection to the Father's Work

Following this man's miracle, the religious leaders question this man and his parents concerning his blindness and healing. They don't believe his story and so they throw him out of the synagogue.

> Jesus heard that they had thrown him out, and when he found him, he said, "Do you believe in the Son of Man?"
>
> "Who is he, sir?" the man asked. "Tell me so that I may believe in him."
>
> Jesus said, "You have now seen him; in fact, he is the one speaking with you."
>
> Then the man said, "Lord, I believe," and he worshiped him. (Jn. 9:35–38)

The next step is to make a connection to the Father's work by pointing people to Jesus.

Jesus didn't merely give this man his sight and leave it at that. Rather, he stirs curiosity within the man through the miracle of healing. Jesus met a need in this man's life, revealed his own identity, instilling in the man a desire to know God. As a result, the man put his faith in Jesus.

When you minister to the needs of unbelievers, it can eventually instill in them a desire to know God. If it's a miracle, like the blind man's healing, they might turn to God immediately. In this case, time elapsed between the miracle and the man's salvation. Jesus didn't bring him to a decision at the time of his miracle, although he could have. But softening a sinner's heart to the gospel sometimes takes time.

As you love people, show them kindness, and minister to their needs, God can open their hearts to their need of him. Then we can eventually tell the person about Jesus and possibly see them come to faith in Christ.

This is how we let our light shine before men, that they may see our good deeds and praise our Father in heaven (Matt. 5:16). The praise they will give is more than mere verbal praise. God wants our hearts. This praise comes from a heart that turns to him. When people see the good deeds you do for them, they're more likely to turn their hearts to God, as this blind man did.

In Matthew 9:8, we read about the healing of a paralytic. "When the crowd saw this, they were filled with awe and they praised God." The people saw Jesus's good deed and gave God the glory. And in Matthew 15:31, we learn that Jesus performed many miracles. "The people were amazed and they praised the God of Israel." They too saw Jesus's good deeds and gave God the glory. Both verses are examples of others seeing good deeds and praising God for it.

Reaching unbelievers begins with meeting their personal needs through natural means. This brings supernatural intervention, which can lead to their salvation.

We also make a connection to the Father's work by taking Jesus to people.

This is an important element of evangelism because Jesus didn't call the lost to church. He called the church to the lost and the lost to himself. Our goal is to lead people to Jesus, but we must first take Jesus to them. We do that by letting our light shine before them by the good we do for them—by ministering to their needs. I believe we would have more success in evangelism if we focused on leading unbelievers to a person more than to a place: to Christ before church.

When the Holy Spirit was poured out on the day of Pentecost, 3000 people came to Christ. I believe Peter's sermon, along with the fact that they heard them speaking in their own language, contributed to these people's salvation. But so did the people's experience of seeing Jesus's miracles day after day. They saw the blind receive sight. They saw the deaf hear, the mute speak, and the dead raised to life. Jesus's ministry laid the groundwork. Then when they heard these people speaking in their own language and listened to Peter's message, they were cut to the heart and came to faith in Christ.

Years ago, while working as a city bus driver in Spokane, Washington, I had to wait at the bus plaza, which was the hub for connecting different bus routes, to take over for the first driver. I decided to start coming to the plaza early so I could look for people who might need or appreciate a free slice of pizza. I bought a stack of gift cards, and every day, I looked for two people to give a card to. I wanted to meet a need in people's lives (many were homeless or poor) and to build a relationship with them. I would tell them Jesus loves them, cares for them, is always there for them, and wants them to reach out to him.

After leaving my job as a bus driver, I continued going downtown once a week, where I handed out breakfast burritos and told people about Jesus. Whether I gave pizza gift cards or breakfast burritos, people saw the love of Christ. They were more open to the gospel, and some responded by putting their faith in him. I still enjoy the privilege of ministering to the homeless.

In 1989, the Lord first opened my eyes to this passage and principle. It was from this passage that he began giving me a vision for my life. I had a grasp on the principle of reaching the lost through ministering to their needs, but eventually this took on fresh meaning at a new level.

It's important to note that Jesus ministered to people one on one. He didn't go to the crowds. The crowds came to him. After Jesus healed Peter's mother-in-law, many demon-possessed people were brought to him that evening (Matt. 8:14-16). Jesus healed one person and as a result, many others were brought to him. I have a vision for reaching many people in greater quantities. But I also know that reaching many begins with reaching them one at a time.

Jesus also reached people on their own turf and in their own environment. He reached them where they were. Taking Jesus to people requires that we do the same. We must minister to people one on one right where they are.

You can do the same in everyday life as you look for ways to minister to people's needs by natural means. God will use you in greater ways, and you will live each day with greater purpose.

Reflection

1. How can I make my contribution to the Father's work?
2. What "natural means" can I use to impact others?
3. Who can I impact, using those natural means?

Encouragement: Evangelism takes on a new dimension when you love people by meeting their needs. We must show the love of Jesus before we can share the love of Jesus. Loving people isn't confrontational. It isn't about shoving the gospel down anyone's throat. It's simple and doable.

Challenge: Look for needs in others' lives, no matter how small the need. When you find a need, meet it.

Prayer: *Dear Lord,* open my eyes to the needs of others, and give me wisdom to meet those needs. Help me to make the most of every opportunity with the resources you have given me. In Jesus's name, amen.

Chapter Eleven

Stepping into God's Supernatural Provision

"About this time next year," Elisha said,
"you will hold a son in your arms."

2 Kings 4:16

2 KINGS 4:8–37

$\mathcal{E}$ach of us has a hope, dream, vision, or promise from God for our lives. We look to God because he is the only one who can provide it. Our *vision* becomes God's *provision* when it is fulfilled. Some of you have waited a long time for God to fulfill your dream. Maybe you've prayed for years for that one thing to take place. I know I have. What you are waiting for is a breakthrough for whatever you're longing for to become a reality.

Your God-given vision for your life, the dream or desire inspired by God goes through a process before becoming a reality. When it does become a reality in your life, you will be stepping into God's supernatural provision.

For the sake of clarity, I'll use the word *vision* to include your hopes, dreams, passions, desires, and promises of God.

We all must take a six-stage journey before we can see our vision fulfilled:

- Inspiration of a Vision
- Conception of a Vision
- Preparation of a Vision
- Creation of a Vision
- Termination of a Vision
- Resurrection of a Vision

Inspiration of a Vision

> One day Elisha went to Shunem. And a well-to-do woman was there, who urged him to stay for a meal. So whenever he came by, he stopped there to eat. She said to her husband, "I know that this man who often comes our way is a holy man of God. Let's make a small room on the roof and put in it a bed and a table, a chair and a lamp for him. Then he can stay there whenever he comes to us."
>
> One day when Elisha came, he went up to his room and lay down there. He said to his servant Gehazi, "Call the Shunammite." So he called her, and she stood before him. Elisha said to him, "Tell her, 'You have gone to all this trouble for us. Now what can be done for you? Can we speak on your behalf to the king or the commander of the army?'" She replied, "I have a home among my own people." "What can be done for her?" Elisha asked. Gehazi said, "She has no son, and her husband is old."
>
> Then Elisha said, "Call her." So he called her, and she stood in the doorway. "About this time next year,"

Elisha said, "you will hold a son in your arms." "No, my lord!" she objected. "Please, man of God, don't mislead your servant!" (2 Kgs. 4:8–16)

The inspiration of a vision is birthed when you release your resources to meet someone's need.

The Bible says this woman was well-to-do, so she had the means to give Elisha food, shelter, and a place to sleep. But if she hadn't provided for Elisha, he wouldn't have returned the favor. She provided for him, so he wanted to do something for her.

This woman most likely had a dream and desire to have a child or children, probably early on in her marriage. However, given her response to Elisha, she probably had long given up on it. Now her inspiration to have a child is renewed. The inspiration of a vision for having a child traces back to her helping meet Elisha's needs.

Having a place for Elisha to stay while he was in this area of the region was obviously a need in his life or the woman would not have done it for him. Elisha greatly appreciated it, or he would not have returned the favor. This is a kingdom principal: When we do for others what they can't do for themselves, God does for us what we can't do for ourselves.

This woman was wealthy, but we can all do something to help meet others' needs, no matter our economic status. We can give financially, or we can give of our time and service.

One of my earliest recollections of being inspired to go into ministry was when my wife and I began working in the children's ministry of our church, Valley Assembly of God. My heart's desire was to reach families that did not go to church. So, we started a bus ministry where we picked up children in the community and brought them to our children's church service. We would then visit these families during the week to build a relationship with them. It was a ministry that others had started in the church prior to this, which we were involved in at one time, but had since died out. So we restarted the ministry when we took over the children's church service. During this time the Lord placed a call upon my life to make ministry my vocation. That inspiration came from seeking the Lord and serving others in this bus ministry.

In the early years of our marriage, my wife had two miscarriages. After that, we became foster parents of young children. One was a six-week-old baby, straight out of the hospital. He was in the hospital so long because he needed to get through his fetal drug addiction. We had him for over three months, and it was difficult to let him go. This made us want our own children all the more.

We took care of several children over those few years. Then the Lord blessed us with two of our own. He used those miscarriages to lead us to becoming foster parents. Then, because we did for those kids what they couldn't do for themselves, God did for us what we couldn't do for ourselves: conceive and give birth to two healthy children.

Conception of a Vision

At the conception of a vision, we get a picture of the impossible.

At first, this lady said, "Don't toy with me now and get my hopes up. Are you serious about this? Because my husband is old, and I gave up on that dream a long time ago." Her situation, in natural terms, was impossible. But now she got a picture of something she never thought possible, something she gave up hope for many years ago.

Abraham's wife Sarah was barren until God gave her a child. Her miracle happened when she was ninety and Abraham was one hundred years old. There was no way that was going to happen by natural means. If Abraham and Sarah could have made that happen on their own, they would have done so a long time ago. Now, given both their ages, it was impossible. But God made possible what was impossible by them.

When God gives us a vision for our lives, it's going to be impossible for us to carry out on our own. It was true for this woman as it was for Sarah. It's also true for my life as well. When God first gave me a vision for my life, it looked very doable to me. Not until the Lord gave me a greater revelation of the vision did I come to believe it was impossible for me.

If you have a vision for your life that you think you can accomplish, it's probably not God's vision for you or, like me, you have not come to a complete understanding of it. When God gives us a vision for our lives, it should scare us. It should cause us to say, "There's no way I can do that." Because in reality, we can't, not without God doing it in and through us. That was my response when I came to fully understand God's vision for my life. I knew it was something only he could do. I knew there was no way I could bring it about on my own.

If God has given you a hope, a vision, or a promise for the impossible, don't doubt its validity or possibility. He specializes in the impossible. When he gives us hope, a vision, a promise, a dream, or a desire, we must allow him to bring it to pass in his time. What is conceived of God is always impossible for us to fulfill on our own. Believe God for the impossible.

What impossible desire has God placed in your heart? Do you want something that only God can give? Get a picture of the impossible for your life.

Preparation of a Vision

> But the woman became pregnant, and the next year
> about that same time she gave birth to a son, just as
> Elisha had told her. (2 Kgs. 4:17)

The preparation of a vision is a season of growth in your life.

The preparation of a vision is the incubation period when development takes place, much like a child in the mother's womb. It's a stage of development and growth, not only for the vision growing in you, but for you as well.

During this season, you may experience tests, trials, temptations, and even pain, suffering, isolation, and loneliness. How do I know? I've had to deal with all those things while waiting for my vision to come to fruition. I can look back now and see how God used that season in my life (and still does) to grow me and prepare me to carry out his plans for me. I can also see how the devil tried to steal, kill, and destroy that vision.

You can be sure a battle rages for the vision God has for you. Satan will attempt to derail you, but God will protect and empower you as you stay close to Him.

That's why it's important to make Jesus, not the vision, your priority. In this season, seek the Lord in greater measure. God is honing you, maturing you, and developing the vision within you.

As time goes by, the vision grows until it's a central focus in your life. You may even become obsessed with it. You live, eat, breathe, sleep the vision. You anticipate its arrival as a mother awaits the arrival of her child. You prepare for it.

You will probably even try to make it happen on your own. But God allows no premature births of his vision for your life. If you try to make it happen on your own, you'll only get frustrated.

There have been times in my life where I've started a ministry, hoping and praying that "this" might be it. "Maybe this time I'll cross that threshold. Maybe this time I'll get my breakthrough." But none of those times resulted in what I was looking for. Why? Because it wasn't time for the fulfillment of the vision. That's not to say that I was trying to force the vision into reality. I was, however, "knocking" on certain doors to see if any one of those were the specific time and place God had in store for my vision to become a reality.

Let God develop you as well as the vision within you. We can't rush this stage of development and growth. If we birth the vision too soon, its chance of survival decreases. Be patient and rest in the fact that God is at work, and his timing is perfect.

Creation of a Vision

During the creation of a vision we begin to see the unfolding of the vision.

The Shunammite woman gave birth to her son. Finally, she saw the fulfillment of God's promise given to her by Elisha a year ago. Remember, in her mind this desire for having children was long dead and gone. Now, here she is holding God's "supernatural provision" in her arms.

The very thing that God has placed in your heart for your life and future will, at some point and time, begin to take on substance. You will see it take form. It will develop right in front of you. You will have every indication that it's a matter of time until it becomes a reality. To some degree, you will have a "taste" of the vision. There will be every indication that it's here or at least well on its way and will only grow from this point forward.

Through the years as an evangelist, I've attempted to relaunch my ministry on several occasions. I held a three-day revival in the small town of Ione, Washington. It went well, but when it ended that was it. I've attempted to get speaking engagements in different churches. I've ministered to the homeless. I tried putting together a youth rally that never transpired. I've made many attempts at ministry.

One such ministry began when I was driving a city bus. I began a weekly evangelistic service at the bus plaza on Saturday nights. My son, along with a worship team, began each service with worship. As the music played, people would begin to make their way to find a seat and listen to the music. There were already many people at the plaza, so getting them there wasn't a problem. Following the worship I would give a short salvation message.

When I first started our Saturday night evangelistic services, we had just conducted our first service. The next morning, on Sunday, I had a speaking engagement at a church in the Spokane area. I had given a message and gave testimony to our new ministry launch and what the Lord had done the night before with people coming to faith in Christ. Following the Sunday morning service my wife and I met for lunch at a local restaurant, since she attended our home church that day. While I was waiting for her to arrive, suddenly my eyesight went double. It was so difficult to see that I had to sit down and close my eyes. Every time I opened them, I was seeing double. Someone from the church that I normally attend, came up to talk to me, but I had difficulty even looking at him. It lasted about ten minutes and my eyesight returned to normal. It was the oddest thing, right out of nowhere. I knew right then it was an attack of the devil.

Right after that my wife came into the restaurant. I told her what had happened, and so after lunch she took me to the local urgent care. They sent me promptly to the ER at the hospital thinking I may have had a stroke. I told my wife that it was just a fluke, that it was just an attack of the devil because of what just took place in both Saturday night and that Sunday morning services. To make a long story short, they ran tests on me at the hospital with follow up tests the following week or two with different doctors. Nothing was found to have caused the problem. There was no evidence of even a minor stroke. They had no answers for me.

What I know to be true is that when you begin moving into new territory, especially the enemy's territory, he will bring an attack on your life. That attack is not confined to the spiritual realm. It can come in different forms, even physically like it did for me. You can be sure that you're on the right track when you start running into the devil himself.

We continued our evangelistic services. Every week there were those who would invite Jesus into their lives. Things were going great. I could envision it becoming a fruitful ministry in the heart of downtown Spokane. This was the creation stage of God's vision for my life. It was becoming a reality right in front of me.

You may have experienced something similar yourself. You may even be there right now. Everything is on track. The signs are there. You can see it unfolding right before your eyes. You can see things coming together. The adrenaline is starting to flow. Your hopes are at an all-time high. Even though you may have experienced the attacks of the enemy, it looks as if this is it and nothing can stop it now.

Termination of a Vision

> The child grew, and one day he went out to his father, who was with the reapers. "My head! My head!" he said to his father.
>
> His father told a servant, "Carry him to his mother." After the servant had lifted him up and carried him to his mother, the boy sat on her lap until noon, and

then he died. She went up and laid him on the bed of
the man of God, then shut the door and went out.
She called her husband and said, "Please send me one
of the servants and a donkey so I can go to the man of
God quickly and return." (2 Kgs. 4:18-22)

When she reached the man of God at the mountain,
she took hold of his feet. Gehazi came over to push her
away, but the man of God said, "Leave her alone! She
is in bitter distress, but the Lord has hidden it from me
and has not told me why."

"Did I ask you for a son, my lord?" she said. "Didn't I
tell you, 'Don't raise my hopes'?" (2 Kgs. 4:27–28)

A vision must die before it can live.

Jesus said that, unless a seed falls to the ground and dies, it
will not bring forth life (Jn. 12:24). A seed must die before it can
become a plant. So it is with your vision. It must die before it can
become what God wants it to become.

Everything was moving forward as planned for our Saturday
night evangelistic services at the bus plaza in downtown Spokane.
Then, out of nowhere, our ministry ended abruptly. They decided
to remodel the plaza, which meant we could no longer use the area
where we had been conducting the services. The vision that was
becoming a reality right before my eyes was suddenly gone. Even
after the remodel was completed, we were not able to restart what
we had before due to policy changes at the plaza.

The same will be true for you. At some point your vision will
die. You won't know what went wrong, because the failure doesn't
make sense. You'll feel devastated, frustrated. You'll question God
and yourself.

Prior to the ministry at the bus plaza, I experienced the death or termination of my vision while pastoring Suncrest Family Worship Center in Nine Mile Falls. I had a unique experience where I could see my vision becoming a reality. I could see myself standing on the threshold of God's vision for my life. I could see the vision becoming a reality before my eyes, and it was then that God removed me from ministry altogether. There were no circumstances to dictate my resignation. On the contrary, my ministry there was an incredible joy from start to finish. Nonetheless, God made it clear to me and told me it was time to step down. It didn't make sense to me or anyone else for that matter. But it doesn't have to. God has the big picture, and he knows what he's doing. During those years following my resignation, I held different positions in different companies. Each one a learning experience. Each one a ministry in itself. How does a person hang on for so long waiting for the vision to become a reality? It has its ups and downs, for sure. It can be frustrating at times and to a certain degree fulfilling. You look for ways to be useful where you're at. No matter what, through it all, you can try to let go of the vision, but the vision won't let go of you. Deep down inside you continue to hope because of the vision God has given you.

Resurrection of a Vision

> Elisha said to Gehazi, "Tuck your cloak into your belt, take my staff in your hand and run. Don't greet anyone you meet, and if anyone greets you, do not answer. Lay my staff on the boy's face."
>
> But the child's mother said, "As surely as the Lord lives and as you live, I will not leave you." So he got up and followed her.
>
> Gehazi went on ahead and laid the staff on the boy's

face, but there was no sound or response. So Gehazi went back to meet Elisha and told him, "The boy has not awakened."

When Elisha reached the house, there was the boy lying dead on his couch. He went in, shut the door on the two of them and prayed to the Lord. Then he got on the bed and lay on the boy, mouth to mouth, eyes to eyes, hands to hands. As he stretched himself out on him, the boy's body grew warm. Elisha turned away and walked back and forth in the room and then got on the bed and stretched out on him once more. The boy sneezed seven times and opened his eyes. (2 Kgs. 4:29–35)

Necessary steps are required to resurrect the vision.

Even though we've been looking at this passage from the perspective of the woman's vision, a transition takes place here where Elisha takes it on as if it were his own because of his personal involvement from the start. So, what we learn from Elisha we can apply to our own lives.

Interestingly, the first thing Elisha tried, instructing Gehazi to lay his staff on the boy's face, didn't work. He took a step of faith; he acted, but it didn't work. Remember, this is Elisha, who'd performed many miracles. But this initial failure didn't stop him.

He implemented a new strategy. He laid on the boy, and then he walked back and forth, probably praying. He took a prayerful step, and he took a practical step. He prayed, but he didn't just pray. He also took a practical step by laying on the boy. The miracle still didn't happen immediately.

When Elisha entered the room, he "shut the door on the two of them and prayed to the Lord." Sometimes when we need God to step on the scene and do what only he can do in our situation, we just need to go to the Lord in desperation on our own. There's a time when we need others to pray with and for us in our situation. But there is also a time when we just need to keep others out of the equation and seek the Lord until our answer comes. The vision God has for your life is between him and you. Some things are only going to come about because God is waiting for you to get to a place of depending solely upon him and not others. It's up to us to take the initiative in prayer and practical steps.

When the miracle did come, this mother's son was returned to her.

If your vision has died, ask yourself how badly you want it. Are you willing to see it through, to do the work required? Are you willing to go the extra mile by praying and taking necessary steps toward a breakthrough? Like Elisha, just because one attempt failed, are you going to keep trying? I had to ask myself those very questions. And in answer to those questions, I have taken extra steps to one day step into God's supernatural provision for me.

As I discussed earlier, I enjoy handing out food to the homeless in downtown Spokane. As a result, God has blessed me in many ways, but that's not why I do it. I merely want to give back to God and to minister to lost people. In a sense, it fills my longing for ministry. Contributing to kingdom work gives me a sense of satisfaction. It's my practical step toward resurrecting the vision.

Along with that, I began seeking God in greater measure for a breakthrough. I've been combining prayer and practical steps to seeing my breakthrough take place.

I wasn't trying to force God's plan in my time. But after you've walked through the process, seeking the fulfillment of your vision, and God stirs your heart, you can be tenacious about moving forward to see your vision fulfilled.

I wish I could tell you the story of how God has resurrected his vision for my life at this time, but I haven't seen the evidence of that yet. I know it's coming soon, which is why I'm preparing myself for it by continuing to seek the Lord in greater ways and taking practical steps toward it.

Reflection

1. What has God put in your heart to believe him for?
2. Where do you see yourself in this process?
3. What is your next step toward God's supernatural provision for you?

Encouragement: No matter where you are in this process, God is working everything out in his perfect time. He has a plan, a purpose, a promise, and a vision for your life.

Challenge: Choose to trust God's hand working in the details of your life. Relinquish control so he can lead you toward fulfillment of the vision he has placed in you.

Prayer: *I believe, Lord,* that you are actively involved in every detail of my life. Help me to follow you in obedience to your will and your ways as you fulfill your vision for my life. Show me where I am in this process of your vision for my life and the steps I need to take from here. I trust you fully with my life and my future. Thank you for all you have done for me and are yet to do. In Jesus's name, amen.

Chapter Twelve

My Life Through This Process

Thirty years ago, the Lord gave me a vision for my life and ministry, which at the time wasn't clear. But as the years passed, the vision became clearer. It was as if the vision were developing within me. During those early years I felt God calling me to the ministry.

As I worked on my studies, preparing for the ministry, I also continued to work full time outside the church while raising a family and doing volunteer ministry in the church.

Years down the road, the Lord opened the door for me to go into full time ministry, which eventually led to pastoring my own church. One Sunday morning during my time at Suncrest Family Worship Center, I had a fresh encounter with the Holy Spirit.

Sitting on the front row of the church, I listened to the worship team as they practiced prior to the Sunday morning service. Suddenly, I felt such a powerful presence of God, I began to weep uncontrollably. How was I going to preach in this condition? I certainly couldn't talk to anyone before the service. I stayed where I was, sitting in the front row as people entered and the service began. When it came time for me to step onto the platform, I finally pulled myself together and managed to preach.

From that day forward, I felt I had an anointing that would change my ministry. With this turning point, I believed my vision would finally become reality. I had a renewed passion for ministry and seeing myself stepping into God's supernatural provision after all these years.

Then the Lord told me it was time to step down. He even made it clear that he was removing me from the pastorate.

The church didn't want us to go, but they understood. My family had been down this road before, so they were willing to make another change.

I made plans to start my own ministry as an evangelist, thinking that was how the Lord would fulfill my vision. After all, I had the heart and calling of an evangelist. A very generous man and friend of mine in the church, C. J. Lovik, made it possible for me to start my own nonprofit, which I still have to this day. But no matter what I did, I could not get my new ministry off the ground. I got very few speaking engagements. I planned events and started a ministry, all of which seemed fruitful at the time, but they didn't evolve into anything. No ministry, no financial support.

The vision was dead.

Finally, I had to let it go.

The Lord gave me one particular passage to explain what had happened to me since my "heavenly encounter" at the church and what I was presently experiencing. It was Jesus's baptism and temptation, found in Matthew 3:13–4:11. After Jesus's baptism, the Holy Spirit descended upon him. Then where did he go? Did he step into public ministry after his heavenly experience? Did he start his 501(c)(3) and put together a board of directors? Did he start a website and Facebook page to get the word out that his ministry was about to begin? Surely, that would have been the perfect time. He'd just been baptized in water. The Holy Spirit had descended upon him, and the Father had spoken to him in a personal yet public encounter. It looked like the perfect time to launch his ministry.

But that's not what happened. Instead, the Spirit led him into the desert, into a wilderness experience, where he would suffer hunger and temptation and isolation from human contact. He would undergo a battle with the devil himself, fighting for his Father's calling. Following that wilderness experience, "Jesus returned to Galilee in the power of the Spirit" (Lk. 4:14), and his public ministry began.

Once the Lord made clear to me that I was undergoing a similar process (like other's in Scripture and maybe yourself), my life over these past years has made more sense.

Now, over twelve years after leaving the ministry, the Lord began reviving the vision in my heart once again. He has begun stirring a renewed hope for the resurrection of the vision and my return to ministry. I still don't know what that will ultimately look like, but I'm taking the next steps.

During those early years of ministry, followed by twelve years of being out of the ministry, I have applied all the principles discussed here. They have proven to be true to life. God has used them to direct my life all these years and will continue to do so.

God promised his people, the Israelites, the land of Canaan. He told them that he was going to give them that land. Not only did God tell them he had this land for them, not only did he tell them where it was, he also described it for them. He said it was a "good and spacious land" (Ex. 3:8), a land "flowing with milk and honey" (Ex. 3:17). Why did God give them a description of the land? Why didn't he just tell them where it was and leave it at that? It's because he wanted to instill a vision in the hearts and minds of his people for what he had for them. He not only gave them a promise of the land for them, he gave them a vision for it. It was up to the Israelites to follow the Lord in faith and obedience, to consecrate themselves, to fight to possess the land, to live in holiness and relationship with God in order to conquer and continue to live in the freedom of enjoying that land.

After the Israelites had been in the promised land, some tribes having already taken possession of their portion of land, "there were still seven tribes who had not yet received their inheritance" (Josh. 18:2). So Joshua said to the Israelites: "How long will you wait before you begin to take possession of the land that the Lord, the God or your fathers, has given you?" (Josh. 18:3). The land was theirs to possess, but these seven tribes hadn't taken the initiative to possess what was rightfully theirs. God had already given it to them, but they had yet to possess it.

So it is with us. God has more life for you to experience in him. He has given us the freedom, the victory, his gifts, every spiritual blessing in Christ, and whatever your need is. You just need to take possession of it as you live out these principles. God will take you where you've never gone before to do what you've never done before in him.

Chapter Thirteen

One Final Word

*T*here's a truth that I want to make very clear. The Christian life is not about us. It's not about getting God to make our lives more enjoyable. He's not a vending machine or a genie in a bottle to give us what we want. It's not about what God can do for us or even what we can do for God. It's about what God has already done for us by providing for the forgiveness of our sins so that we can live in a love relationship with him. It's about Christ in you (Col. 1:27). Jesus is the center of the gospel. We are not. We live in a love relationship with Christ, walking out his plans for our lives as he lives in and through us.

With that in mind, the Christian life is not always an easy road to walk. On the contrary, there are trials, temptations, suffering, difficulties, and hardships along the way (Acts 14:22). There is more to this life, but more often than not, getting there requires experiencing the pain that comes with it. Yet through it all, Jesus is there to help you, strengthen you, encourage you, challenge you, and uphold you. Look to him in all your difficult seasons of life. You can still experience the fullness of life in Christ in the midst of your pain and suffering. It's through pain and suffering that we find "more" to this life in a closer walk with Christ.

Cry Out to God

One morning, several years back, I had a dream of a worship service taking place. The leader was singing a song that I'd never heard before. I immediately woke up from the dream and it was morning. The only part of the song that I heard in the dream was the chorus and melody. I only knew some of the words that I quickly wrote down before I forgot them. I then began to write the words to the verses that I did not hear in the dream, but what I felt the Lord was leading me to write. I then worked out the chords on my guitar to the melody that I heard in the dream. I'm including the words to this song at the completion of this book because one of the lines in the song, "There is so much *more to this life*," included the title I gave this book, which didn't occur to me until later.

The title of this song is "In This Moment." It's based upon the blind beggar in Luke 18:35–43. When the blind man heard the crowd going by, he asked those around him what was happening. They told him, "Jesus of Nazareth is passing by." The blind man called out to Jesus. This was his moment for a miracle, and he wasn't about to let Jesus pass him by. He was in a desperate place.

Here are the words to that song that seem to coincide with some of the areas discussed here. Make them your heart's cry if you are in need of God's intervention "in this moment" to experience more to this life.

In This Moment

There are many lost in this world,
Who are dying in their sin.
There are many saved in this life,
Who are called their souls to win.
There are many who cannot see,
That their greatest need is Him.
There is so much more to this life,
For those God lives within.

Lord, I need you in this moment,
So please don't pass me by.
May it be here in this moment,
That I see you in new light.
Let it be here in this moment,
That your touch restores my life.
Lord, I need you in this moment,
So please don't pass me by.

There are many who in this life,
Are hurting deep within.
There are many who are suffering,
That need your healing to begin.
There are many without answers,
In the hopeless state they're in.
Lord, I know that this is true you see,
Cause I am one of them.

Lord, I'm praying in this moment,
With all of my might.

To fill me with your Spirit,
Display your power in my life.
I'm crying out to you Lord,
Turn my darkness into light.
Lord, I seek you in this moment,
Please help me in this fight.

Lord, I need you,
How I need you. (3x)

No matter where you are in your walk with the Lord, no matter how mature you are in your Christian faith, no matter what you've encountered in your past, there is still more to life in Christ than you currently experience. There is still more land to conquer, more of God's love to experience and share, more souls that need saving, more life to experience in him.

I hope and pray that the principles laid out in these pages will help you to experience more life in Christ as you live out the life God created you for.